# CONTRA COSTA COUNTY

*Produced in cooperation with the*

*Concord Chamber of Commerce*

*"Contra Costa County's Enterprises"*

*by Hal Straus*

# CONTRA COSTA COUNTY

## *A Chronicle of Progress*

*by John Leykam*

*Frontispiece by Bob Rowan/Progressive Image*

*Windsor Publications, Inc.*
*Northridge, California*
*Windsor Publications, Inc.—History Books Division*

*Managing Editor: Karen Story*
*Design Director: Alexander D'Anca*

*Staff for Contra Costa County: A Chronicle of Progress*
*Manuscript Editor: Marilyn Horn*
*Associate Editor: Jeffrey Reeves*
*Photo Editor: Robin Mastrogeorge*
*Editor, Corporate Biographies: Brenda Berryhill*
*Production Editor, Corporate Biographies: Una FitzSimons*
*Editorial Assistants: Didier Beauvoir, Thelma Fleischer, Kim Kiev-*
*    man, Rebecca Kropp, Michael Nugwynne, Kathy B. Peyser,*
*    Pat Pittman, Theresa J. Solis*
*Publisher's Representatives: Dave Cook, Liz Cook*
*Layout Artist, Corporate Biographies: Bonnie Felt*
*Layout Artist Editorial: Robaire Ream*
*Designer: Marianne Gladych*

*Library of Congress Cataloging-in-Publication Data*
*    Leykam, John.*
*    Contra Costa County : a chronicle of progress / by John*
*    Leykam ; "Partners in progress" by Hal Straus ; produced*
*    in cooperation with the Concord Chamber of Commerce. —*
*    1st ed.*
*        p.   cm.*
*    Bibliography: p. 187*
*    Includes index.*
*    ISBN 0-89781-289-1*
*    1. Contra Costa County (Calif.)—Economic conditions.*
*    2. Contra Costa County (Calif.)—Social conditions.*
*    I. Concord Chamber of Commerce (Calif.)*
*    II. Title.*
*    HC107.C22C665 1989                    88-28696*
*    330.9794'63—dc19                         CIP*

*Windsor Publications, Inc.*
*Elliot Martin, Chairman of the Board*
*James L. Fish III, Chief Operating Officer*
*Michele Sylvestro, Vice President Sales/Marketing*

*In recent years the city of Rich-*
*mond has concentrated on im-*
*proving its container port and*
*on refurbishing its downtown,*
*and in doing so has generated*
*new interest in the city's busi-*
*ness and residential communi-*
*ties. Photo by Mark Gibson*

# CONTENTS

New horizons of prosperity and
growth await Contra Costa County.
Photo by Bob Rowan/Progressive
Image

# FOREWORD

Contra Costa County: A Chronicle of Progress is a sparkling, vivid testimony to the greatness this county has attained in a relatively short period of time.

In text and pictures, this book portrays the ongoing, multifaceted effort to enhance the quality of life in Contra Costa against the backdrop of continuing major economic development.

All the chapters take a fair and realistic look at the challenges confronting the county. Tribute is paid to individuals and organizations inherently connected to this stirring story of achievement.

Contra Costa County: A Chronicle of Progress is a celebration of our accomplishments in the past and a preview of even brighter things to come for the county in the years ahead.

Dr. Ronald L. Stewart
Contra Costa County Superintendent of Schools

This impressive volume, Contra Costa County: A Chronicle of Progress, tells an inspiring story: the story about how this county became one of the finest places in America to live and work.

John Leykam, the author, depicts with lively detail the many favorable attributes of Contra Costa. He gives the county personality by tracing the efforts of individuals who have helped make our region so outstanding.

This book accomplishes what it sets out to do. Conclusions are drawn about the future of the county by careful examination of both the past and the present.

Contra Costa's progress story is a never-ending one. Achievements chronicled herein will hopefully prove the catalyst for the county to attain even higher levels of accomplishment in the years ahead. That, I know, is the hope of all of us.

Sunne Wright McPeak
Contra Costa County Supervisor representing the Greater Concord Area

*Mist rises from the waters at Indian Valley as dawn breaks over Contra Costa County. Photo by Roc DeWilde*

10

# ACKNOWLEDGMENTS

The author would like to acknowledge the extensive input of the following persons to the text of this volume:
—Albert Compaglia, former chairman, Contra Costa County Planning Commission.
—Alex Mehran, president of the Contra Costa Council, 1986-1988.
—Brother Dennis Goodman, FSC. Archivist, Saint Mary's College.
—Dean S. Lesher, chairman and publisher, Lesher Communications, Inc.
—Edward Del Becarro, Cygna Development Company, Walnut Creek.
—George Gordon, founding father of the Contra Costa Community College District.
—Harry York, executive vice president, Concord Chamber of Commerce.
—Paul Hughey, former executive vice president, Contra Costa Council.
—Jack Horton, retired executive vice president, Richmond Chamber of Commerce.
—Sunne Wright McPeak, Contra Costa County supervisor.
—Worth Shaw, recreation director, Antioch.

*Although farming is slowly declining in Contra Costa, a small group of farmers continue to make a profitable living. Charming rural vistas and lush fields are a common sight in the eastern section of the county. Photo by Meri Simon*

# INTRODUCTION

*1333 North California Boulevard in Walnut Creek, constructed by Prometheus Development, is one of many impressive modern office structures in Contra Costa. Photo by Bob Rowan/ Progressive Image*

**I**f they could see it now, the early settlers of Contra Costa County—determined men and women of a wide range of ethnic, personal, and occupational backgrounds—would be bowled over by the complexity and dynamism of their cherished county.

Those early settlers could not have imagined today's sleek and swift commuter trains; crowded freeways with, at some points, five lanes of traffic in each direction; and huge office parks, futuristic in form, with state-of-the-art technology.

Housing of every conceivable shape, size, and price range is available to accommodate a population that grows larger and more diverse each day. In addition to Bay Area Rapid Transit, highway improvement has aided county residents in reaching their destinations.

Pacific Southwest Airways' initiation of scheduled service between Los Angeles and Concord's Buchanan Field in the spring of 1986 gave the county a window to the world via connecting flights at Los Angeles International Airport. The acquisition of PSA by USAir in 1988 made long trips even easier for travelers from Contra Costa. Made possible by PSA's working agreement with Northwest Orient Airlines, the timetable for the new Concord service included listings of such far-off destinations as Tokyo, Japan, and Cancun, Mexico.

Railroads have long played a significant role in moving people and products through Contra Costa. Still, those early settlers would surely get a kick from seeing the double-decked Amtrak Superliners that leave Martinez daily on treks throughout the country.

From very humble but sound beginnings, the county's infrastructure has matured by leaps and bounds. Transportation is just one example. There are numerous others: schools, leisure activities, and retail offerings.

To fulfill their need for a wide spectrum of goods and services, Contra Costa residents no longer have to rely on metropolitan areas to the west. Likewise the county's early settlers did not go far from home in quest of the essential staples of life—but for different reasons. Virtually everything they needed was near at hand.

The influx of thousands upon thousands of new residents to this enchanting portion of the East Bay has not dimmed the spirit of community and camaraderie so prevalent among Contra Costa's pioneers. Little towns of the 1800s have been replaced by large cities of the late 1900s. In homeowners' associations, service clubs, church groups, and youth organizations, present-day county folks find the friendships and networking opportunities they need.

Evolution of the Contra Costa private sector into a region envied by chamber of commerce presidents nationwide has spawned numerous groups dedicated to the advancement of professions or timely issues. Accountants, car dealers, insurers, real estate salespeople, and the media all have countywide or regional trade organizations which bind them together and promote their interests.

In both the private and public spheres, many women hold positions of leadership in the county. In fact, compared to areas of similar size, Contra Costa has a high percentage of female city council members. Chambers of commerce—located in virtually every Contra Costa community and entrusted with the responsibility of representing the diverse elements of their memberships—have had women presidents on a regular basis. Professional businesswomen's associations have enjoyed widespread acceptance. So, too, have organizations targeted to people of specific backgrounds, such as the Contra Costa Black Chamber of Commerce and the Contra Costa Hispanic Chamber.

Though their names may have been changed in some cases (i.e., Black Diamond to Pittsburg), the county's cities have managed to maintain their distinctive charms while tearing down the walls of provincialism.

The Contra Costa Council, formerly the Contra Costa Development Association, has proved to be an effective bridge between businesses from all parts of the county. A nonprofit group dedicated to seeking solutions for the challenges presented by rapid economic growth, the council possesses a membership representing a wide range of interests. Its list of former presidents is a "Who's Who" of individuals who have paved the way for a better county.

"We are dedicated to coming up with answers to the crucial questions that confront Contra Costa today," said Alex Mehran, developer of San Ramon's Bishop Ranch, who guided the council for two presidential terms during the late 1980s. "The goal of simply attracting new business to the county is not where we're at anymore."

The attention that Contra Costa's progress has received from such notable publications as the *Wall Street Journal* and the *San Francisco Chronicle* is testimony to just how far the county has come in the period of a few decades. To understand the present, however, one must investigate the past and the forces that brought the area to the headline-making point it is today.

Contra Costa's early settlers, including Spanish rancheros, Italian fishermen, and Welsh miners, encountered an area with pretty much the same geography, topography, and favorable weather conditions we are blessed with today.

Statuesque Mount Diablo, its Spanish appellation (Devil Mountain) befitting a peak of such massive proportions, reigns proudly over the county. Fertile land and warm temperatures—then as now—create an ideal environment for agriculture. Waterways that for centuries have provided Contra Costa with gateways to San Francisco Bay are of strategic as well as commercial importance.

The series of rolling hills and valleys that distinguish and separate the county from its Bay Area neighbors create a breathtaking setting that will continue to attract new residents and corporations in the future. The concrete caverns of the big cities are seemingly worlds apart from the landscaped office parks that transplanted white-collar workers have found awaiting them in Contra Costa.

Climate, geography, and topography had much to do with the way the county developed in the twentieth century. These factors, combined with strides in transportation, continue to dictate the maturation process today.

Waterways and, later, railroads, provided passageways for raw materials and products essential to operation of heavy industry. Pastoral acres, available in lots much larger than is the case now, created an ideal setting for planting crops and raising livestock.

Cattle still graze on the hills near burgs like Clayton, Danville, and West Pittsburg. These tranquil scenes are very isolated remind-

*Graceful horses run along the*
*rolling hills of San Ramon.*
*Photo by Roc DeWilde*

ers of how simple and sleepy life in Contra Costa used to be. The long-held premise that the county's rolling terrain had only limited useful-ness has been overturned in recent years by proposals to con-struct housing units or entertainment facilities on the hillsides. As could be expected, the tussles over such designs have often been dra-matic.

Heavy industry, symbolized by aging and changing manufactur-ing plants mostly in east and west Contra Costa, has been a visible part of the landscape since the turn of the century. De-spite the dwindling of its ranks in the latter part of the 1900s, heavy industry remains—and will remain—an important cog in the county economy. Cutbacks in the local operations of steel, paper products, and chemical companies, though severe during the last couple of decades, were predictable at least in the

short-range view. Huge complexes like the C&H sugar refinery in Crock-ett have successfully adapted to change.

Modernization of oil refineries in and around Martinez has given these big employers a fresh optimism with which to battle in-creased competition. The era of high technology has spawned a new definition of manufacturing in Contra Costa.

Circuit boards, bits, and bytes are no longer terms that the pen-insula area of Santa Clara County has a lock on. High-tech manufacturers—the likes of Systron Donner, Varian, Zehntel, and Nicolet—have grabbed the chance to locate significant plants in Contra Costa. Research and development of futuristic products occur in the county within such diverse fields as food testing, computer software, and health care. Aiding this challenging, ongo-ing process is the county's proximity to prestigious colleges and universities— "think tanks" for the nation's corporations.

Improvement in technology has also enabled county farmers to reap a respectable return on what they sow—a potpourri of vege-tables as well as fruits and nuts. A diminishing breed, these farmers have implemented new equipment to make their jobs more fluid and rewarding.

As housing developers have made large purchases of land in the east county, especially in Brentwood and Oakley, farm and grazing tracts have gone the route of the cotton gin. Nonetheless, like heavy industry, agriculture has secured a lasting place in Contra Costa's economy. Those farmers and grazers who remain have been rewarded for their hard labor and willingness to adjust in a time of changing technology.

Besides good weather and favorable location, there have been other factors that have had a momentous impact on Contra Costa. A major military presence exemplified by expansion of the Naval Weapons Station at Concord during this generation and by feverish activity at Camp Stoneman in past generations has made history and jobs for the region.

The Second World War's tumultuous effect on the county included such developments as a shipbuilding boom in Richmond; the addition to Saint Mary's College of a naval pre-flight school; the use of Buchanan Field as an important military air base; and a swelling of the population at Camp Stoneman.

Owner of thousands of acres at Concord, the navy (and, in turn, the federal government) qualifies as one of the most prominent landlords in Contra Costa. The employment created by the weapons station for the civilian population is significant in peace as well as wartime.

Contributions made to the county's quality of life by former servicemen and women are numerous. Current naval personnel can be found involved in a myriad of community causes and organizations. Their adopted county has benefitted from their efforts.

The real ballooning of the county's population began in the middle to late 1960s. Luring new residents to cities like Concord and Walnut Creek were very affordable price tags on single-family homes—many of them in the category of four digits. For the middle class, those were the good times in Contra Costa. Home ownership was within reach of even one-income families and job availability was on the rise.

Neighborhoods, echoing with the voices of young children, emerged seemingly overnight. In Concord, for example, Holbrook Heights, Sun Terrace, and Cambridge Village became sections of the city synonymous with the population boom—each with a separate sense of community and shops and schools to serve them.

Even with the opening in 1937 of the Caldecott Tunnel that connected Contra Costa with Alameda County, the region east of the bore remained more of a summer vacationland than a home to most people. The perceived longer distance from San Francisco to this county than to places like the peninsula or Marin, combined with Contra Costa's agricultural reputation, slowed population expansion for several decades.

As counties on the other side of the Bay became built up and Alameda took off in terms of attracting new residents and businesses, Contra Costa quietly prepared for its growing season. Highways improved and the frequency of commuter bus service to San Francisco increased. Supermarkets and retail stores also grew in number.

The "majors," as astute observers of the retail world term the likes of Sears, J.C. Penney, Montgomery Ward, and Macy's, took early note of what was happening in Contra Costa. Hardly had the 1950s begun when J.C. Penney and Sears opened stores in Walnut Creek's budding Broadway Plaza. In Pleasant Hill and Richmond, Montgomery Ward had stores up and running prior to the opening of Concord's Sunvalley Shopping Center in 1967.

Sunvalley's construction on former marshland was a blockbuster signal that the county had indeed arrived. The Michigan-based Taubman Company, a frontrunner nationally in ownership and operation of regional shopping centers, was convinced that the county possessed the household incomes and population to support that kind of mall. Their foresight proved right on the money. Sunvalley has become one of the most prosperous shopping centers in the West.

The swift increase in the county population and tremendous upswing in commercial activity predictably put strain on crucial infrastructures like transportation, housing, schools, energy, and sewage facilities. The inability, perfectly understandable, of these services to stay ahead of the breakneck economic development continued

*Children abound in the county's many neighborhoods, playing catch, riding bicycles, and skipping through yards.*
*Photo by Meri Simon*

A spring rainstorm passes
over the Richmond-San Rafael
Bridge. Photo by Jordan Coonrad

into the 1970s. Citizens' dissatisfaction with mounting traffic and
other not-so-nice effects of expansion surfaced in ballot measures
in Concord and Walnut Creek to contain growth. The results of
the votes were mixed. The same can surely be said for the range
of opinion on how big Contra Costa should ultimately become.

Just as the Caldecott Tunnel gave Contra Costa much-
improved access to Alameda County (and vice versa), completion
of the Richmond-San Rafael Bridge in 1956 and the Martinez-
Benicia Bridge in 1962 opened the county's "window" to Marin
and Solano counties.

The importance that railroads have had in the growth of
Contra Costa cannot be minimized. Though there has been a
gradual dwindling over the last few decades in the number of
lines and trains that move passengers and freight through the
county, railroads continue to be crucial to the area's progress.
The Southern Pacific and Santa Fe carry not just oil but a wide
variety of goods to destinations throughout the nation. Amtrak,

with depots in Richmond, Martinez, and Antioch, draws a great
number of passengers from Contra Costa.

Whether the county would have developed as dramatically as
it has without the presence of one very special railroad is doubt-
ful at best. Bay Area Rapid Transit, the futuristic and frequently controversial commuter railroad which links the East Bay to San
Francisco, opened the county up to commercial expansion in a
way that its predecessors in the people-moving business could
not. Up and running in the late 1970s, BART preceded by only a
few short years the rapid construction of office space in central
Contra Costa. Corporate decision-makers, convinced of BART's
general efficiency and magnetized by relatively cheap (compared
to San Francisco) land and rental costs, transferred significant operations to the Concord-Walnut Creek corridor in the early 1980s.
Not surprisingly, many of these office complexes cropped up
within walking distance of busy BART terminals—i.e., Central
Bank's headquarters in Pleasant Hill and Bank of America's data processing and technology center in Concord.

Business and government leaders from the Antioch-Pittsburg-
Brentwood area have pulled out virtually every stop in trying to
bring actual BART rail service to their borders. Realization of such
a dream, they are convinced, would bring significant economic benefits. And despite the fact that their regions have prospered
without the presence of BART trains, officials from the Tri-Valley

The very distinctive features of different portions of the county lend themselves to particular kinds of business. Thus there will always be agriculture in Brentwood and heavy industry along the waterways near Pittsburg and Martinez.

Undoubtedly, however, the principal element of Contra Costa's economic growth saga in the future will be service companies, particularly in the areas of finance, insurance, and real estate. Decisions by well-known firms—like Bank of America, The Travelers, McMasters and Westland Commercial Real Estate, Chevron, 1st Nationwide Insurance, Wells Fargo Bank, and Reynolds and Brown (Real Estate)—to situate significant operations in the county will be a catalyst for maintenance of that trend.

Sophistication has rapidly become a hallmark of Contra Costa—one which serves as a magnet for prestigious corporations to settle here. "These firms want to be in good company. They like what they see happening in the county," said James Bailey, long-time area retail manager for Bank of America. Household income levels in Contra Costa qualify it as one of the wealthiest counties in the state and nation. Educational levels also say a lot about the kind of new residents the area is attracting.

As additional big-name companies relocate here, the reverse commute of people from other regions to Contra Costa will become even more apparent. The flip side of the extra pressure such a trend will signal for county roads is the very positive increase in service and retail businesses responding to the needs of an expanding private sector. There is good and bad with rapid economic development, county residents have come to learn.

Prompted in part by corporate relocations, but also fueled by enlargement of existing, county-based businesses, Contra Costa has quickly become a popular place to work for individuals from throughout the Bay Area and beyond. Whopping increases in the number of people who live and work in the county have qualified Concord, Walnut Creek, and the cities immediately surrounding them as an "urban village."

No longer, say authorities on socioeconomic matters, does this cluster of communities depend primarily on San Francisco for employment of its residents and for important human services. The 1980 Census, which revealed that 60 percent of Contra Costa residents work in Contra Costa, underscored that shift.

The many millions of dollars that corporations have invested in moving complexes to the county and parallel increases in the white-collar residential population have led to a generally higher quality of life in the region when compared to even just a few years ago.

Well-regarded restaurants, hotel chains, specialty stores, and professional groups have all found Contra Costa a profitable place to do business. Entertainment is now close to home as exemplified by the name performers being booked at the Concord Pavilion and Rheem Theater. With Walnut Creek Civic Arts, the Dramateurs of Lafayette, and other county performing arts organizations, there is plenty of opportunity to enjoy local talent. And, if fate proves kind, the county could soon have a regional performing arts center.

Flourishing of the urban village in and around Concord-Walnut Creek had dramatic, ongoing implications for the communities located within a half-hour drive of it. Benicia, Martinez, Pittsburg, Antioch, and Hercules have become bedroom communities to their larger neighbors. The presence of regional shopping centers in Con-

in and around San Ramon know its importance. Sunset Development's establishment of its own bus service between Bishop Ranch and the Walnut Creek BART terminal exemplifies that sensibility.

Increasingly trouble-free BART service between the county and the downtowns of San Francisco and Oakland has enabled Contra Costa residents in increasing numbers to forsake their autos and avoid such nagging bottlenecks as the 680-24 freeway interchange. Topographical barriers that, for decades, separated the Richmond area from the rest of the county have been bridged by BART trains.

Where would central Contra Costa be today without BART seems a very valid question given the county's progress since its start-up. The striking reality of a reverse BART commute of San Franciscans to places like Pleasant Hill, Walnut Creek, and Concord goes a long way in providing an answer to that intriguing inquiry.

Variety is a vivid attribute of the county today. Its private sector is bolstered by just about every type of enterprise imaginable. The fast-growing population is a conglomerate of various ethnic and social backgrounds as well as income levels. Fortunately the brisk economic development of the last few decades has helped foster the diversity that has allowed the region to profit considerably in good times and weather difficult periods in far better shape than its neighbors.

cord (Sunvalley) and Walnut Creek (Broadway Plaza) is a large part of the magnet which draws outlying residents to the central county. All kinds of retail outlets, including fine line and discount stores, have sprouted in the urban village. Since so many of them work there, east county residents and others list Concord-Walnut Creek as a primary setting for purchase of durable goods.

While people in high places try to find funding for major transportation improvements, the county closes in on the 800,000 population mark—a milestone it will reach in the 1990s.

Contra Costans have learned that there are things they can do to alleviate the congestion on local highways. Van and car pools, flex time, and shorter workweeks have been experimented with to ease the sometimes dire traffic situation. Despite fare increases, BART ridership has stayed relatively stable.

The proliferation of buses to move people within the county, especially to BART stations, has been a very noticeable sign of the county's growth. The Central Contra Costa Transit Authority ("County Connection") and Tri-Delta Transit in the Antioch-Pittsburg corridor have been aggressive in their campaigns to get people to ride the bus. Yet old habits are difficult to reverse. Until that time when freeway interchange bottlenecks are eliminated, roads are widened, and the Caldecott Tunnel receives a new bore, the one-rider vehicle will remain a major obstacle to smooth people-movement.

Pressure on mass transit agencies to increase ridership is heightened by the economic development of outlying areas where relatively affordable housing prices cause residential populations to swell. In several "senior cities" of Contra Costa, the long view of decision-makers is to establish a significant source of white-collar employment within their boundaries. Not surprisingly, then, aging downtowns have been spruced up in hopes of paving the way for a renaissance of business.

Martinez, home to John Muir, birthplace of Joe DiMaggio, and the seat of Contra Costa government, long went unnoticed by outsiders. The very early retail hub of the county has accomplished significant economic progress in the last decade, however, due largely to construction of significant research and development complexes along Highway 4, emergence of a scenic waterfront park, and much-needed improvements on Main Street.

Those frequenting the Amtrak station on Ferry Street have a wide variety of restaurants and shops available to them. The echo of whistles from tankers berthed nearby is a reminder that the oil industry is still very much alive and well in this historic city.

New home construction on the west side of Highway 4 has widened the scope of Martinez and prompted the emergence of new neighborhood shopping centers which sweeten the municipal tax base. The rediscovery of the city by the outside world is a most intriguing element of the county's maturation.

Not too far from Martinez, good things are also happening in the west county—not just in Richmond but also in burgs like Pinole and Hercules. Blessed with room to grow, an overall positive feeling toward development, proximity to San Francisco and Highway 80, and a wide range of housing stock, the region is making people and companies stand up and take notice. The beneficiary, naturally, of this upswing is the ethnically diverse population of Richmond and nearby cities.

As it has for decades, Chevron's manufacturing and refining plant at Richmond is the bulwark of the west county's economy. Im-

proved and modernized several times over, it provides employment for thousands of residents of nearby and distant communities. But beware of the pitfall of believing that the area has only a single-focus private sector. Even Chevron has spread its wings in Richmond and ventured into other endeavors, producing Ortho garden products there. The now multidimensional city has nurtured an impressive flower- and plant-growing industry and serves as home to the celebrated Color Spot company.

The waterfront has always been an important part of Richmond. In the 1980s the city expended massive sums on developing a first-class container port that would give San Francisco and Oakland a run for their money. Though progress was predictably slow at first in securing users for the port, its long-range potential for success is very good. With the Pacific Rim reputed to pay a high yield for West Coast cities in the near future, Richmond is well-positioned.

While a feverish redevelopment process is succeeding in giving Richmond's downtown a new look, transportation in and out of the area has improved dramatically thanks to construction of freeways that shorten the trip to Interstate 80. Encouraged by what they see, businesses are taking fresh interest in Richmond. The Taubman Company's decision in 1975 to locate a regional shopping center, Hilltop, in the city was the impetus for growth of the surrounding vacant land—nearly a thousand acres total. A most diversified tract, Hilltop now has offices, an auto dealership park, research and development facilities, and small professional businesses in addition to the shopping mall. Pinole, Hercules, and other west county cities have profited from Richmond's resurgence. Located relatively close to both Marin and Solano counties, they can be expected to prosper even more in ensuing decades.

Less than a half-hour's drive from the west county on the San Pablo Dam Road lies Lamorinda. The wealthy triumvirate of Lafayette, Moraga, and Orinda—because of location—cannot detach itself from the dramatic development encompassing Contra Costa.

Residents of these luxurious bedroom communities, with comfortable homes selling in the high six figures, continue to draw their wealth from the other side of the Caldecott. Nonetheless these cities have carefully and in some ways inconspicuously forged their own economic identity. In doing so, they have centered their efforts on assimilating professional and value-oriented retail businesses into their midst.

The shift of the county away from a largely agrarian society is perhaps best exemplified by what has occurred in the Tri-Valley that straddles Alameda and Contra Costa along Highway 680. Bishop Ranch, the nearly 600-acre development of the Mehran family, will be home to nearly 25,000 employees when it is built early in the 1990s. Household-name firms such as Toyota, Chevron, Pacific Bell, and Marriott have found the erstwhile pear and walnut plantation an ideal location for warehousing, office, and hotel facilities. The San Ramon spread has also become home to an impressive educational cooperative shared by several institutions of higher learning.

Opening of Stoneridge mall by the Taubman firm and dramatic successes by Hacienda Park in attracting impressive office tenants have put nearby Pleasanton on the map in a big way. Commercial development of the valley has paralleled significant residential expansion. Relatively quickly, Alamo, Danville, and Blackhawk have established themselves as among the most posh addresses in the Bay Area.

Business and government leaders in the south county have adopted an aggressive posture in meeting the challenges stemming from rapid growth. With cooperation from the private sector, not to mention large chunks of money, the young city of San Ramon has attacked the traffic problem head-on. During his two terms as president of the Contra Costa Council, Alex Mehran led the fight to try and increase sales taxes to help fund transportation improvements.

Very little farming still goes on in the Tri-Valley. However, about an hour away in the east county the pungent smell of crop fertilizer is unmistakable. Along Highway 4 on the way to Stockton, fields of green can be seen for miles. A variety of crops means an uncertain but a usually profitable mode of existence for a dwindling number of farmers.

Their scenic domain has been substantially whittled away in the last several years by developers who bought up large sections of former pastureland on which to build single-family homes. The bargain prices they got were passed on to mostly young, first-time buyers in the form of affordable dwellings with backyards for growing families.

Oakley, an unincorporated community east of Antioch, and the city of Brentwood are on the horizon of Contra Costa's future. There, new homes in great numbers seem to rise from the once-pastoral sod almost weekly. To serve them, shopping centers with name tenants have emerged. Antioch and Pittsburg are not quite ready, though, to pass on the gauntlet of expansion to their smaller neighbors. The two former smokestack cities still have land on which to build more homes and businesses. By some experts' calculations, Antioch will eventually be the second-largest city in the county (after Concord), with a population of nearly 100,000 people.

The need to diversify an economy dominated by heavy industry is probably best typified by events at the US Steel Pittsburg Works—employer of more than 4,000 workers in its heyday in the mid-century. Ravaged by the popularity in the last few decades of lower priced Japanese steel, the Pittsburg plant and its blue-collar force took a nose dive. Employee numbers were cut by more than half. A subsidiary, Antioch Bridge, was shut down. Reverberations of these gloomy happenings were felt throughout the east county. The wisdom of a region being economically diversified was starkly demonstrated. During the late 1980s, a Korean steelmaker, Posco, joined forces with US Steel in hopes of reviving the sprawling steel plant. To that end, the Oriental company was willing to invest millions. How successful this well-publicized effort will be is yet to be determined.

In the meantime, leaders from the east county have tried to stabilize their industrial base comprised of a combination of chemical, paper products, and gas companies. They also have heightened their bid to gain actual BART rail service—a development, they believe, that would attract new white-collar businesses and major retailers.

Well aware that new residents are headed their way in droves, these decision-makers are also trying to ensure that medical facilities, schools, and sewage plants can meet much-increased demand.

*The lush hills of Moraga create a striking silhouette at dusk. Photo by Bob Rowan/ Progressive Image*

The blending of old and new is unmistakable in the Concord-Walnut Creek urban village of the late twentieth century. True, the vegetable farm whose spectacular view once delighted freeway travelers through Pleasant Hill has been replaced by Ellinwood—a massive development of homes, offices, and restaurants. But Todos Santos Park in downtown Concord and Main Street in Walnut Creek conjure up enough memories of yesteryear to keep any historical society happy. Businesses like Lehmer's Oldsmobile in Concord span the generations. There are many others that do likewise.

Streets, schools, and parks have names that provide a glowing chronology of the way the region has progressed. Futuristic, mid-rise office buildings, many adorned with reflective glass, point to the heavens. On the blocks beneath them, well-maintained homes of early 1900s vintage stand proud—and occupied.

Handsome, state-of-the-art medical facilities aptly named John Muir and Mt. Diablo are enlarging and becoming even more sophisticated in the services they offer. The Contra Costa Community College District annually sends many of the graduates of its three campuses to prestigious colleges and universities nationwide. Saint Mary's College of California tripled enrollment in less than two decades.

The maturing of Contra Costa always has been eventful, trying, and rewarding. It is a progress story with hundreds of important postscripts waiting to be written. It is a story with no end in sight. To those wistful for the way the county used to be, I say don't despair. There will always be enough intermingling of the old and new in Contra Costa to give substance and meaning to the present.

Above all, be thankful for those early pioneers who gave us our start. For their foresight, hard work, and wisdom, we shall forever be indebted.

# PART ONE

# A MODEL OF AMERICAN ENTERPRISE

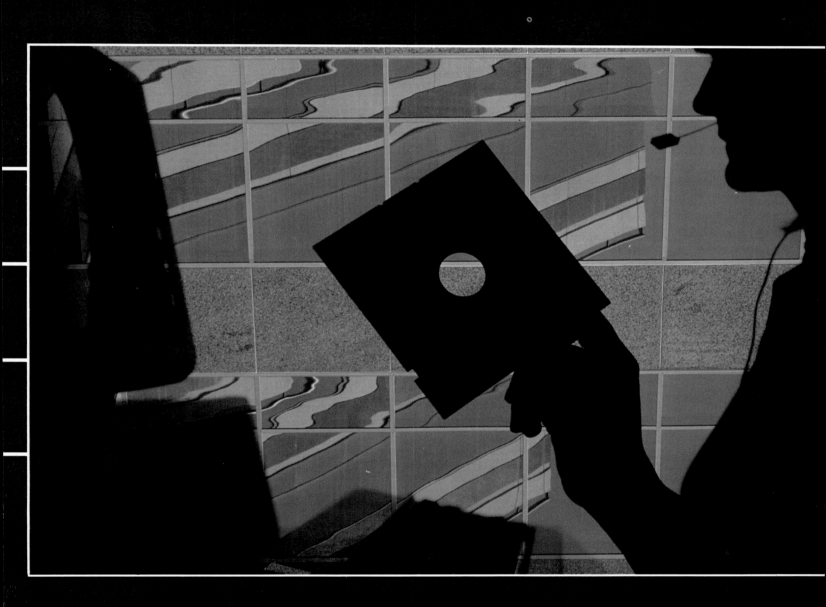

The computer industry provides a major source of employment opportunities for the county's white-collar workers. Photo by Bob Rowan/Progressive Image

# CHAPTER 1

The staff of the Henry W. Bott Black-
smith and Wheelwright shop of Concord
proudly posed at their place of business
in 1874, around the time the establishment first opened. Besides serving as black-
smiths, these men also built wagons and
ran a machine shop. Courtesy, Contra
Costa County Historical Society

# A HISTORICAL PERSPECTIVE

In the continuing saga of the San Francisco-dominated Bay Area, Contra Costa is often relegated to the position of the "new kid on the block."

National and regional publications can be excused for zeroing in on the last few decades of the county's long history. The economic development unfolding here beginning in the late 1950's is the kind of stuff from which lead stories are made.

Nonetheless the extensive attention given to the present has come at a cost of short-changing the past. For the annals of Contra Costa are resplendent with events and personalities of lasting significance.

Fortunately, groups and individuals have recognized the value of preserving the county's rich heritage so that their successors to this land can enjoy and learn from it. Historical societies thrive in several Contra Costa communities. A number of cities have erected museums to house artifacts of bygone eras.

Names that are well known to local residents—names like Castro, Martinez, Moraga, and Pacheco—serve as testimony to the fact that the county's roots run long and deep. Timetables from railroads which crisscrossed the breadth of Contra Costa early in this century mention hamlets now existing only in memory. Each had a special identity; a separate role to play in the maturation of the region. Among those bygone communities were Saranap, Selby, and Valle Vista.

Electric and steam railroads and ships of all sizes and uses opened the county up to the rest of California and the world. As it does today, Contra Costa stood at the crossroads for people venturing into Northern California. For countless men and women en route elsewhere, the county would prove to be a starting rather than stopping point.

The Hispanic influence on Contra Costa—portrayed by such lasting appellations as Rodeo, Mount Diablo (one of the Bay Area's highest points), and Martinez—was extensive. The county's enchanting topography, with rolling hills, rivers, and valleys, was a magnet to early Mexican settlers whose family trees could be traced back to Spain.

Ranchos, owned and ruled by Hispanics, were the appropriate setting for large-scale agricultural endeavors. There was a pioneer spirit attached to the time (1769-1848) when California was ruled by Spain and Mexico.

The origins of this now very modern county go further back than the rancho period, however. For centuries before the arrival of the Spanish, Indians inhabited the territory later to be named Contra Costa.

These native Americans, who occupy a special place in the state's history, were caretakers of our pastoral landscape. Their survival hinged on hunting, fishing, and gathering.

Distinctly different tribes inhabiting the future Contra Costa area included the Yokuts, Bolbones, Miwoks (Saklans), Suisunes, and Costanoans. Each had its own territory. For the most part, these tribes lived in harmony with one another.

With Catholic missionaries and the military playing ever-larger roles in the settlement of Northern California in the late eighteenth and early nineteenth centuries, the Indians quietly faded from importance. They did not receive proper recognition until many years later.

In 1848, following Mexico's independence from Spain and the subsequent takeover of Mexico's northern territories by the United States, gold was discovered in the Sierra foothills.

Victory by the United States over Mexico, coupled with the Gold Rush, set off a massive migration into California of people from all parts of the

*Facing page, top: Local residents stroll along Ferry Street in Martinez in 1908. Courtesy, Contra Costa County Historical Society*

*Facing page, center: Martinez was chosen as the county seat in 1850 when Contra Costa County was officially established. In this 1890 view, looking west, the county courthouse is visible near the center of town. Courtesy, Contra Costa County Historical Society*

*Below left: Concord's first electric railway car arrived in February 1911 on the Oakland-Antioch Railroad line. The advent of railroads provided a direct link between Contra Costa and the rest of the state. Courtesy, Contra Costa County Historical Society*

*Below: Contra Costa's local Indians belonged to the Penutian family and consisted of many different tribes. The most common dialect spoken was the Saklan dialect. As depicted in this illustration, fishing and hunting were the main sources of food and activity for these Indians. Courtesy, Contra Costa County Historical Society*

country and the world. Serving as a gateway to San Francisco and the Pacific, Contra Costa would never be the same again.

Frustrated gold seekers found a promising refuge in this county, which, during the early era of California statehood, included the city of Contra Costa—soon to be renamed Oakland.

Entry of California into the United States and the need to resolve ownership of former Mexican-held lands set in process the first population explosion in Contra Costa. Although land titles granted by the Mexican government were deemed to be valid, American squatters soon claimed the unfenced rancho lands as their own. Most rancheros eventually lost their property, but some adjusted to—and even encouraged—Americanization.

Landlord Vicente Martinez instructed his brother-in-law, William M. Smith, to oversee construction of a town on the west side of El Hambre Creek which poured into the Carquinez Straits. The resultant community of Martinez quickly became a transportation hub for gold miners and for delegates to the constitutional conventions in Monterey, San Jose, and Sacramento. Primitive ferries took great numbers of Americans between Martinez and Benicia. Stage lines were established in Martinez, from which the rough-riding coaches were dispatched to such far-off cities as San Jose and Oakland. Discovery of coal in the hills above Clayton spurred the founding of what would prove to be Martinez's most enduring stagecoach business.

Trains first started running through Martinez in 1876, opening the community to another wave of settlers. In addition to becoming the county seat, Martinez would receive notoriety by being home to Contra Costa's first newspaper (the *Gazette*), to fabled Scottish-born naturalist John Muir, and to the Christian Brothers' Novitiate and Junior Seminary. Beginning in 1905, the city would evolve as a center for oil refining.

*Right: The Shell Oil Company built a refinery in Martinez to serve its oil fields in Coalinga to the south. The plant opened in 1916 and has successfully expanded its services over the years. The refinery, pictured here under construction in 1915, is still a thriving industry in Contra Costa County today. Courtesy, Contra Costa County Historical Society*

*Left: The Martinez City Wharf was a vital aspect of the town's early years of economic growth. Courtesy, Contra Costa County Historical Society*

*Below, center: The townsite of Somersville, pictured here in 1878, grew up in the hills of Mount Diablo during the coal mining boom of Contra Costa County. When mining reached its peak in the mid-1870s, Somersville boasted a population of about 1,000 and was one of the largest communities in the county at that time. Courtesy, Contra Costa County Historical Society*

Communities like Richmond, Antioch, and Pittsburg were shaped by the dominating influence of their waterfronts. The potential for effective, seagoing transportation of raw materials and finished products was a magnet to early industrialists and mining companies.

Richmond, a relatively late entry into the growth scenario enveloping Contra Costa, became a scene of frenzied business activity around the turn of the century. The start-up in 1901 of Pacific Coast Oil Company's new Richmond refinery was a key event in the city's history. The transfer of the manufacturing complex to Standard Oil in 1906 secured Richmond's role as a leading industrial center of Northern California. The massive Chevron facility which today straddles the shores of San Francisco Bay is clear evidence of the role oil plays in the city's present and future.

The Santa Fe Railroad helped fuel Richmond's initial boom by locating extensive repair shops and a ferry terminal there. Financial institutions like the Bank of Richmond and Mechanics Bank were created to respond to the needs of varied businesses including brick, pottery, and steel-making plants. During the lifespans of succeeding generations, Richmond would acquire a reputation for being the site of Pullman train car construction and a full-speed-ahead shipbuilding effort that helped bring the United States to victory in World War II.

Contrasting to the development of Richmond, the Delta towns of Antioch (formerly Smith's Landing) and Pittsburg (formerly New York Landing and Black Diamond) originated during the 1850s. Coal transformed

these east county communities into a bustling economic complex of major proportions. Its discovery led
to the establishment of Nortonville, Somersville, and Stew-
artsville, and formation of a transportation network encompassing narrow-gauge railroads and oceangoing schooners.

The early settlers of Pittsburg and Antioch who
did not engage in mining found livelihoods in farming, fishing, and small industry. In time, both towns would
spawn other businesses including canneries, steel
plants, and lumberyards.

The value of waterfront property is perhaps best demonstrated by the prosperity that came to the tiny

west county hamlet of Port Costa. In 1879 the Central Pacific Railroad linked the town with Benicia and
points east via a train-ferry. Port Costa, with its deep channel docks, became the loading point for millions of
tons of San Joaquin an Sacramento Valley-grown
grain destined to feed people across the globe.
Hundreds of mammoth schooners frequented the
port, sparking a local economic boom that would last
early into the twentieth century.

Avon, Port Chicago, and other riverfront towns
drew their strength and vibrancy from the rapid proliferation of industry. In the case of Port Chicago, the
military was largely responsible for growth of the community.

Walnut Creek, the hub of regional agricultural activity, and Pacheco, which emerged as a regional trad-
ing center in the late 1850s, were focal points of the county's early development. Concord, the largest and most
populous city in the county for the last several decades, was an extension of Pacheco.

The devastation caused in Pacheco in 1868 by tor-
rential rains and a severe earthquake had residents search-
ing for a place where they could make a fresh start.
Lots were provided free for the asking two miles to
the east of the town. Don Salvio Pacheco, the
grantee of Rancho Monte del Diablo, instructed that a community of 20 acres be formed there. First named
Todos Santos, that community would eventually become Concord. Concord soon was dotted with businesses providing goods and services to farm families
from all over the area.

While Concord was gaining a widespread reputation for retailing, other segments of its economy were be-

ing nurtured. Orchards bearing different fruits covered much of the landscape. Service establishments became increasingly popular and profitable for budding entrepreneurs.

The start-up of the Cowell Lime and Cement Company in 1905—three years after the city's incorporation—proved to be an event of great significance. Within a few years, the company established itself as Concord's largest employer. The massiveness of the Cowell mining operation is perhaps best demonstrated by the fact that it spawned both narrow- and standard-gauge railroads used to transport the thousands of tons of finished products to market. The heyday of the company lasted into the early 1930s.

During the 1980s Concord has maintained and enhanced its reputation for being a commercial center of great renown. Office complexes housing such name tenants as Chevron, C&H Sugar, and Bank of America have given the city's private sector a twentieth-century dynamism to complement its well-established retail and service sectors.

The southern portion of Contra Costa has been the scene of brisk office development during the 1980s. The early history of towns in that area gave not even a hint of a move toward that direction.

Take San Ramon, as an example. Up until the middle of this century, the sprawling acreage that has evolved into Bishop Ranch Business Park was covered with orchards and fields of grain crops. Through most of the early part of this century, livestock and sheep grazed on the hillsides of the very pastoral Tri-Valley.

San Ramon's history, like that of many other county communities, reveals a rich ethnic flavor. Irish farmers became the town's largest landholders in the mid-1800s. At different stages of its maturation, San Ramon carried the names Limerick and Lynchville.

The Irish connection to San Ramon is one of many examples of how Contra Costa became a "melting pot" of peoples from around the world.

Our heritage is filled with reminders of the years that this region was part of the Spanish Empire. Names of towns in the west county—El Sobrante, San Pablo, and Pinole—reflect their Hispanic roots.

Don Salvio Pacheco, Juan Bautista Alvarado, Ignacio Martinez, and Francisco Castro were all key figures in the early history of Contra Costa. Though born in the Americas, they gave to this new frontier a spirit and culture distinctly Hispanic. These trailblazing individuals carved considerable reputations primarily by being land rich. Alvarado was the most politically formidable of the group, having ruled a republic and served as governor.

Gritty men like Pacheco, Alvarado, Martinez, Castro, and Concord pioneer Francisco Galindo effectively bridged the periods of Mexican and American rule. Their influence was enhanced by California's entry into the United States, for they saw to it that American-

ization went as smoothly as possible—land transfers and all.

The legacy of Hispanics in Contra Costa is preserved today by more than city and street names. In keeping with a trend that demographers contend will continue throughout the state, Hispanics have assumed roles of growing importance here. Their clout encompasses both the private and public sectors and is most evident in the east county. There, in the stretch of communities from West Pittsburg to Byron, Hispanics have taken leadership positions in a wide range of organizations. Numbered among the first group of inductees into the Contra Costa Hall of Fame was Pittsburg restauranteur Bill Muniz, a person deeply involved in several humanitarian causes. In the late 1980s, a Hispanic Chamber of Commerce emerged to help further the efforts and interests of Spanish-speaking businesspeople throughout the county.

In addition to the Hispanics and Irish, people of many other nationalities figured significantly in the "growing up" of Contra Costa.

From Martinez to Antioch, fishing became an important industry in the nineteenth century. Men of Italian roots, whose families had fished the seas near Sicily, built their own boats and worked the rivers with great success. At one point, around 1910, an estimated 1,000 Sicilian fishermen were busy in Delta waters. Their huge catches helped establish what would become another key east county business—canning.

Crops nurtured in the fertile fields of Contra Costa were processed and then canned at sprawling complexes purposely situated along rivers to ensure swift transportation of these foodstuffs to waiting markets.

The agrarian pursuits prevalent in all parts of the county during the late 1800s relied heavily on the labors of Scandinavians, Portuguese, and Irish. These hardworking families of European ancestry engaged in farming, ranching, and dairy work. English settlers found livelihoods in agriculture and a wide range of service businesses. East county coalfields prospered, largely due to the dedication and perseverance of Welsh miners.

With California's entry into the Union came a massive migration of people from the East and Midwest. Missouri—because of its central location— became the gathering and "jumping off" point for these hearty pioneers. Not surprising, then, is the fact that many people destined to become important to Contra Costa were born in that state.

The huge influx into the county of peoples from other parts of the United States had already begun when California was still a part of Mexico.

Dr. John Marsh and Elam Brown—who migrated to Contra Costa from Massachusetts and the Midwest, respectively—were key figures throughout the process of Americanization. These two very powerful men bridged the periods of Mexican and U.S. rule and, in the process, reserved for themselves a permanent place in history.

Both Marsh and Brown derived considerable clout from ownership of sprawling territory. Marsh reigned over the 13,316-acre Rancho Los Meganos in the east county until his death in 1856. As a physician and provider of numerous goods and services to area residents, Marsh achieved wide renown. Through published letters expounding on the blessings of California to people in Missouri bivouacs, Marsh served as a one-person chamber of commerce. Such correspondence helped fuel the mass migration westward.

Ownership of a few acres of his property was transferred eventually to the San Pablo and Tulare Railroad Company, and Marsh's memory was rekindled by naming the tract "Brentwood." Not lost on the railroad, obviously, was the fact that Brentwood was the town in England where the Marsh family's roots were.

As a representative to California's constitutional convention, Elam Brown gained prominence on a wide scale. Owner of a huge tract in and around what was destined to become Lafayette, Brown got to this county via a circuitous wagon train route that crossed the then-perilous heartland of America. Brown's son, Thomas, also became a distinguished Contra Costa citizen, serving the public as a judge and surveyor.

Horace Carpentier was another American-born land baron of significant importance to Contra Costa. His five rancho holdings in and around what is now San Ramon were the setting for some of the most fertile agricultural fields in the region.

The evolution of the county into the busy, modern, and prosperous place it is today has launched many individuals and groups into the limelight. Future decades and centuries will undoubtedly produce many more heroes and heroines of Contra Costa.

Very little stays the same in our county. With such dynamism and progress, it is logical to expect that ensuing chapters of our history will be every bit as dramatic as those already written.

*Top, right: Many settlers found steady work as farm laborers in the late 1800s. These two men pause for a break while stacking hay in an Orinda field. Courtesy, Contra Costa County Historical Society*

*Center, right: Eager residents in horse-drawn carriages wait for the incoming Southern Pacific train at the Concord Depot in 1910. The railroad brought prosperity to the area and helped to spur the county's future growth. Courtesy, Contra Costa County Historical Society*

*Bottom, right: An Oakland-Antioch Eastern Railway car makes its way down Hartz Avenue in Danville in 1920. Local towns, such as Danville, continued to expand and develop as more people arrived in Contra Costa in search of a prosperous life on the West Coast. Courtesy, Contra Costa County Historical Society*

*Facing page, top: Alhambra Creek in Martinez was once a small but thriving village that was settled in the late 1800s by Italian immigrants. These people made their living as fishermen, following the spring and fall fishing seasons of the area. Although the community itself has diminished in size and population, feelings of pride for the town's heritage are still quite strong today. Courtesy, Contra Costa County Historical Society*

*Facing page, bottom: Grain farming diminished in Contra Costa after 1890, due to the successful progress of orchard and vineyard cultivation. The first power sprayer available in the county was used at the John Swett Ranch, pictured here around the turn of the century. Courtesy, Contra Costa County Historical Society*

# CHAPTER 2

When professional businesses started to move their offices to the affordable and spacious area of Contra Costa, residential and office development exploded into a flurry of activity, which continues to maintain a fast pace today. Photo by Bob Rowan/Progressive Image

# FACTORS BEHIND THE BOOM

The East Bay, as it is popularly known today, could hardly be considered a frontier. Businesses, homes, and freeways cover most of the landscape as far as the eye can see. Comprised primarily of Alameda and Contra Costa counties, the busy region is a prominent component of the larger, metropolitan Bay Area.

Though there is no longer a frontier in the sense of a scene from a Western movie, there still exists a "Great Divide." The Caldecott Tunnel is more than just the separating line between Alameda and Contra Costa. It heralds the passage from the old to the new; from cool to warm temperatures; and from an urban to a suburban lifestyle.

The crush of vehicles trying to squeeze through the tunnel's three bores during rush hour Monday through Friday testifies to the brisk growth Contra Costa has experienced in the last quarter-century. The relocation of major corporate complexes to the county has caused the phenomenon of an ever-heightening reverse commute away from San Francisco. The private sector's efforts to implement alternative working arrangements like flex time, the four-day workweek, and Saturday schedules have helped ease congestion, but not enough to represent a significant solution to the problem.

Moves to encourage the use of mass transit and van pools, likewise, have been well intentioned but only moderately effective in reducing mounting commute times. The reason is simple: the remedies cannot keep up with

the rising population in cities throughout Contra Costa.

It is true that because of the development of many major office complexes in this county, an increasing number of residents have the good fortune to work within a very short drive from home. The crowded BART trains leaving Concord and Walnut Creek in the early morning hours demonstrate clearly, however, that San Francisco-Oakland will continue to be a source of employment for large numbers of Contra Costans.

Completion of the Caldecott Tunnel in 1937 opened the door for large-scale habitation of Contra Costa by people hopeful of living and/or working here. But as fate and World War II would have it, the buildup of the county's business and residential populations was delayed for several years.

Though anything but serene and sleepy, Contra Costa did not assume a semblance of its present character until the late 1950s. "It was a gradual change; a process that you didn't really tend to notice till the '70s when the big office buildings started going up in Walnut Creek and Concord," said Armand Dianda, a suntanned, energetic senior citizen whose veteran Contra Costa family still possesses extensive land holdings in the county as well as in the San Joaquin Valley.

Dianda is one of a number of longtime Contra Costa residents who find little objectionable in the way the region has developed since the era of the horse and buggy. "Growth was inevitable here as other parts of the Bay Area became filled up," said the mustachioed landowner from behind the wheel of a tractor at his residence in Concord. "Development has brought a lot of good things—better educational facilities, recreational areas, and shopping centers. We would have had traffic problems regardless, since so many people from other areas go through the county on their way to work in the city."

Views from Dianda's Concord property portray the different chapters in Contra Costa's intriguing growth story. Bank of America's mammoth data processing and office center lies about a mile away in the direction of the multistoried downtown in and around Todos Santos Plaza. To the south, Mount Diablo and its pastoral slopes reign proudly over the Diablo Valley. Individually styled residences, as well as tract homes, line the streets where walnut orchards once dominated the landscape. Several times a day, jets can be seen making their descent into Buchanan Field. Train whistles can be heard in the distance.

"I think we have been able to maintain enough reminders of the past to keep us close to our roots," Dianda said. "The high school [Mt. Diablo] where I went still thrives today. There has been a real effort at refurbishing aging buildings and taking pride in the achievements of our pioneer families."

*Above: The Caldecott Tunnel, seen here from the Contra Costa County entrance in Orinda, handles thousands of commuters each workday. Photo by Bob Rowan/ Progressive Image*

*Facing page, top: Offices, homes, and freeways blanket most of central Contra Costa, as illustrated by the sparkling lights of Walnut Creek. Photo by Bob Rowan/Progressive Image*

*Facing page, bottom: The Caldecott Tunnel opened up Contra Costa to the rest of the Bay Area. This view was taken from the Berkeley Hills over the tunnel, with Highway 24 and Mount Diablo visible in the distance. Photo by Roc De-Wilde*

The melting pot that Contra Costa has become—not only of folks from other states, but from other countries as well—has spawned a heritage diverse in ethnic backgrounds, life-styles, and occupations. Opening of the Caldecott Tunnel and the Bay Bridge in the 1930s paved the way for the "Great Escape" of thousands of adventurous people away from the hustle and bustle that—then like now—characterized San Francisco.

The aging Caldecott stands as a monument to the tussle between advocates of growth and no growth. The ongoing debate over whether or not to add more bores to the tunnel at a cost that would go well into the millions of dollars becomes more intense with each rush-hour traffic tie-up at its entrances.

Peter Oswald, a vice president with Sunset Development Company that developed San Ramon's Bishop Ranch, is keenly aware of just how sensitive a topic this is. "Everyone on both sides of the fence would come out of the woodwork on that one," said Oswald, about the recurring idea of putting a fourth bore through the Caldecott. "The issue represents the whole essence of the growth versus non-growth debate—not just on a Contra Costa level but on a regional basis as well.

"To accomplish such a project would require millions and millions of dollars regardless of how the money is raised. Contra Costa residents have demonstrated before at the ballot box their reluctance to increase taxes for transportation improvements. Sure, everybody complains about the traffic, yet the congestion never seems to get to the point where enough

*Above: The blending of diverse ethnic backgrounds has created a strong sense of heritage and history throughout the many towns and communities of Contra Costa. Photo by Meri Simon*

*Left: Splashes of rich green, color the hillsides of Mount Diablo. Photo by Lee Foster*

people are willing to dip into their wallets to really try and turn the situation around."

The six lanes which comprise the Caldecott were plenty sufficient to handle the traffic flow during the first 25 years of the tunnel's existence. Now, many observers of the growth scenario in Contra Costa wonder whether constructing a fourth bore would only be a very temporary fix to a problem in need of a long-term solution.

As forward thinking as they tried to be, very few of the leaders of Alameda and Contra Costa counties could detect the staggering development that would encompass their two-county region in the second half of this century. Little surprise, then, that suggestions for alternate routes to Highway 24 (which cuts through the tunnel) lingered to the point that they became too expensive to be practical. A classic example is "Gateway," the proposed route from Oakland toward southern Alameda envisioned to wind through the bedroom communities of Orinda, Moraga, and Alamo. While wrangling over such a thoroughfare dragged on, home values rose at a rate that made further talk nonsensical.

Although not perfect, Bay Area Rapid Transit has proved the best means of relieving the congestion caused by the Caldecott's inability to accept ever-increasing numbers of commuters in both directions.

Plagued in the beginning by questionable management practices and mechanical failures, BART did not win over a skeptical public until several years after its modest, phased start-up in the mid-1970s. Then, like today, commuters displayed a stubbornness to give up the convenience of their automobiles.

*Right: The Caldecott Tunnel is an integral part of daily life in Contra Costa, handling thousands of commuters each day. Photo by Roc DeWilde*

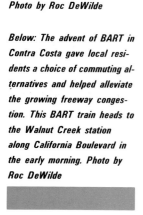

*Below: The advent of BART in Contra Costa gave local residents a choice of commuting alternatives and helped alleviate the growing freeway congestion. This BART train heads to the Walnut Creek station along California Boulevard in the early morning. Photo by Roc DeWilde*

Factors not under their control—rising world gasoline prices and a rising local population which equated to increasing traffic—convinced a significant number of Contra Costans to give the blue-and-silver railroad a try. The cleanliness and quiet of BART was, and is, a refreshing reversal for commuters familiar with the grime, noise, and peril synonymous with subways and commuter trains in places like New York and Chicago.

In becoming successor to Greyhound as the largest mass transit carrier of Contra Costa commuters to San Francisco, BART accomplished what the buses could never do—it took people off the highways. Just how much BART contributed to the buildup of this county is difficult to gauge.

"One thing is for certain: it brought the downtown business districts of San Francisco-Oakland and cen-

tral Contra Costa much closer together," said Larry Westland, a former principal in a commercial real estate firm in Walnut Creek and past chamber of commerce president in that same city. "Companies of all sizes came to recognize the practicality and savings to be realized by relocating certain operations to this county. With the help of BART, executives could get between the metropolitan areas and the suburbs efficiently and quickly without being at the mercy of the Caldecott Tunnel."

Even with fare increases and occasional, well-publicized delays during rush hour, BART patronage remained fairly steady on the Concord line during the 1980s. Hampering increased ridership was an obvious need for additional parking at most Contra Costa stations.

The increase in residential populations of nearby counties such as Solano and Napa also boosted BART ridership and put extra pressure on the system's directors to create more parking space. Part of the endearing attractiveness of places like Benicia and Vallejo—in addition to their affordable housing—is their relative proximity to BART.

With discount home prices a main magnet, eastern Contra Costa experienced a very notable popula-

*Left: Even with the rising cost of fares and parking, BART reaches into many communities such as Orinda, providing an efficient alternative to commuting by car. Photo by Roc De-Wilde*

*Below: Although the cost of housing continued to escalate, the growing population created a strong demand for new housing. The luxurious area of Lafayette features handsome homes, spacious yards, and close proximity to shopping centers and mass transportation. Photo by Bob Rowan/ Progressive Image*

*One solution to the declining availability of land for single-family homes is the construction of additional rental units. Photo by C. Curtis Corlew II*

tion explosion that began in the late 1960s and continues today. Young families with school-age children give a special vitality to the Highway 4 communities of Pittsburg, Antioch, Oakley, and Brentwood. The inevitable increase in housing costs has not deterred that spirit. It has, however, caused a significant heightening of the educational and professional credits of the region's residents.

All of this said, officials in the east county keep waiting and wondering when momentous economic development will occur in their midst—commercial growth of a fervor that began enveloping Concord-Walnut Creek during the early 1970s. One theory has such hopes hinging on the extension of real BART rail service to the area. Nothing less, many feel, will spark a business boom of immense proportions.

Even before the first BART train left Concord on its trek westward, citizen groups in Pittsburg and Antioch were planning where to situate stations in their cities. The lengthy meetings were peppered by intermittent indications that the time for such BART extension was indeed near.

However, as the end of the 1980s drew nearer, hopes became remote at best that the east county or any other area would be getting actual BART rail service in the foreseeable future.

Plagued by rising operating costs and forced—albeit reluctantly—to hike fares, directors of the system were occupied first and foremost with trying to keep ridership at existing levels. Efforts to raise at least some of the multimillions of dollars required for extension of service by delving into the development business were controversial and less lucrative than hoped. The combination of rising fares and the prospect of paying for parking in BART lots was enough to prompt many folks to get back into their cars—even in the wake of spiraling gasoline prices.

The reverse commute of people from the metropolitan Bay Area to jobs in Contra Costa did not pro-

duce the bonanza in ridership BART was expecting. Bus connections to the rail stations were seen by many as too slow and undependable. The prospects for future BART ridership had become so shaky in the closing years of the 1980s that the BART Board was describing the situation in crisis terms.

Emergence of "Park and Ride" lots in the east county that had connecting bus service to the Concord BART station was proof to the region's growing number of residents that actual rail service was, at best, in the distant future.

Tired of the fruitless quest in that direction, private and public sector officials from east Contra Costa poured their energies into seeking a widening of Highway 4, the major thoroughfare from Antioch, Pittsburg, and Brentwood to the central county. That, too, turned out to be a frustrating, tangled waiting game centering around governmental funding delays and the general public's reluctance to agree to tax increases.

Meanwhile, the east county's population continued to swell despite major appreciations of home values. In a span of only about a dozen years, the price of most single-family detached homes in Antioch and Pittsburg nearly quadrupled. That fact notwithstanding, thousands of young and elderly individuals flocked to the area in search of affordable housing.

Inexpensive housing, one of the key factors in the buildup of Contra Costa—especially during the 1960s and 1970s—has long since disappeared. Elected representatives and developers, many of them with offspring of the age to buy their first dwelling, have merged efforts to try and make buying a home affordable for the majority of people.

The result has been an intriguing mix of new residential developments. Condominiums, some of them formerly apartments, became popular for people who because of life-style or financial constraints did not desire the traditional single-family abode.

As residential lots shrank in the face of dwindling developable land, pressure mounted on city halls and home builders to provide more rental units—particularly mid- or high-level apartment complexes. Government officials were reluctant to do so for aesthetic reasons. Builders pointed to the narrow profit margins (compared to single-family homes) and the ongoing struggle to keep units leased. The specter of rent control was very much on the minds of firms approached to handle such projects; they had to look at their potential financial return in a long-term way and apartment construction posed very worrisome questions.

Clark Wallace, president in the mid-1980s of the National Association of Realtors, hails from the western portion of Contra Costa in affluent Lamorinda—the catchy title given to the cluster of towns named Lafayette, Moraga, and Orinda. He is direct about the challenge facing all of the county.

"It's fast becoming a 'dinosaur.' In fact, it is already one in many places," Wallace said when asked about the prospects for affordable housing in the county. "Undoubtedly you will see more and more people checking out the west and east counties and adjoining areas to Contra Costa in an attempt to find the most house for their money. This means longer commutes and increased traffic problems. There are no easy answers to the problem."

Wallace and others close to the home building and real estate industries in the county are hard-pressed to find anything upbeat to say about a solution to the affordability dilemma.

"There's a very high level of awareness about it. At least that can be said," Clark said. "There is an unmistakable urgency about trying to rectify the situation, but there are no quick-fix answers. As the outlying parts of Contra Costa fill up, you are going to see home buyers turn to cities like Fairfield and Tracy to try and settle. What do I mean 'going to see'? That's already begun to happen. Young people have to find help in securing their first home in Contra Costa."

The brisk commercial development of the county, especially in the years from 1975 to 1985, brought with it many thousands of new residents and heightened pressure to greatly expand the housing supply. The age-old relationship of supply and demand, together with the normal appreciation process, combined to put home buying out of the financial reach of many. Not surprisingly, corporations transferring workers to the county from out-of-state had to devise worker-relocation packages that would take into account the tremendous differential in housing prices.

"I remember coming here in 1952 and thinking how I could ever afford my $12,000 home even with a 4 1/2 percent GI loan," recalled Paul Hughey, who served both the Contra Costa Coalition of Business and Labor and the Contra Costa Development Association as executive director. "What houses sell for here now staggers me. But look at the rents. If a person can possibly do it, there are so many more advantages to ownership over leasing. For there to be solutions to this situation, there must be involvement by people and groups with a wide spectrum of interests. There's much at stake in terms of the county's future prosperity and makeup."

The private sector's go-slow attitude toward getting into the mortgage financing business is understandable, particularly with the economic uncertainties of recent years. The county and its cities haven't had time on their side in coping with an outgrowth of the affordability problem: the increasing numbers of county residents who lack the finances to pay for even the most modest housing.

The difficulties experienced by the elderly in trying to keep up with the housing cost spiral were met head-on in cities like Concord with plans to build hand-

*Left: Developing the land for residential, business, and transportation use has created a booming economy in Contra Costa. Neighborhoods have sprung up next to farmland, roads have been constructed to ease the traffic burden, and office complexes have blossomed on vast expanses of land. Photo by C. Curtis Corlew II*

*Right: Housing for senior citizens, such as this complex in Orinda, have been built to provide easy access to the community at an affordable rate. Photo by Mark Gibson*

*Below: Historic Moraga Ranch is a pleasant diversion from the hustle and bustle of daily life. Dating back to the time of the Mexican ranchos, visitors today can explore the renovated buildings, shop in the country store, and sample the sweet, fresh produce. Photo by Roc DeWilde*

some, affordable apartment complexes for senior citizens. These structures were situated in downtown areas where residents would have easy access to stores and professional services.

Escalating housing prices throughout Contra Costa created some interesting sociological changes involving people in their 20s and 30s. Classified sections of newspapers abounded with ads for shared rentals of apartments as well as houses. People had to overlook the fact that they barely knew each other to achieve the urgent objective of putting a roof over their heads.

Parents were getting used to having adult offspring remain in the family residence at advanced ages, even into the early 30s. Reasons for this phenomenon did not involve the desire for family kinship as much as a need to recover from such experiences as college loan payoffs or divorce.

In communities like Orinda, Moraga, Alamo, and Danville, majestic executive homes have always been plentiful. Developments like Round Hill have long been popular to people of upper-income levels because of their detachment from the hustle and bustle of the outside world and their outstanding recreational facilities, most notably championship golf courses.

Nestled in the hills about five miles from Highway 680 and downtown Danville, the Blackhawk tract emerged in the mid-1980s and quickly established itself as the county's model of luxurious living. Controversial baseball manager Billy Martin and the head coach of the Raiders-turned-network commentator John Madden were among those who took up residence in these classy, very high-priced mansions.

Recognizing that not everyone had the vast resources to afford communities like Blackhawk, developers attempted to build homes of which the less financially endowed could be proud. Western Contra Costa became resplendent with a wide-ranging stock of new housing that took full advantage of the area's topographical assets. Burgeoning communities like Hercules and Pinole sprouted from the hilly terrain along and near Highway 80. With inhabitation of these relatively affordable developments, a significant commercial boom occurred involving an influx of retail outlets as well as supermarkets.

Those entrusted with selling the public on the merits of the west county played up its history, changing economy, and nearness to San Francisco and Oakland. Realtors anxiously sought the chance to show people from other parts of the Bay Area the splendid new housing emerging in Richmond. Of particular note were the homes that adorned the rejuvenated marina district in the senior city.

"Low-cost housing and a variety of job opportunities—those two factors as much or more than any other were responsible for the growth explosion in Contra Costa," said Albert Campaglia, a former chairman of the county planning commission.

Compaglia and others remember well—almost like it was yesterday—the time when one salary was sufficient to finance purchase of a traditional single-family home in the county. With price tags for even modest homes in outlying communities going well into six figures, it is no wonder that two full-time salaries are often essential for carrying a mortgage and maintenance of even a medium standard of living. This sociological switch has had major implications for the level of child-care needs in the county.

Task forces to ensure good and affordable child care for the masses cropped up in cities as well as on a county level. Supervisor Sunne Wright McPeak of Concord, herself the mother of two school-age children, made the issue a high priority, personal crusade. "It is a challenge we must address and solve for the sake of our children and the overall fiber of life here," she said.

During the late 1980s, projections on how much employment growth the county would experience during the next decade differed greatly.

There was general concurrence that the majority of new jobs would be of the white-collar, professional variety. The oversupply of office space and the sensitivities of many to further major growth seemed to signal a relative calm in large-scale commercial construction, at least when compared to years immediately gone by.

The near future will be a period of adjustment for a Contra Costa much, much different from even 20 years ago. Urbanization of this formerly suburban and once agrarian county is under way on several fronts.

Residents in every portion of Contra Costa are getting accustomed to riding buses and waiting in traffic. No longer do they have to venture to San Francisco to frequent the most chic of retail stores. Educational offerings and organizations span a wide horizon. Prices for just about everything are in line with the Bay Area's reputation for being one of the most expensive regions in the nation.

All of that does not mean Contra Costa has lost its basic charm or inherent assets. The county's proximity to San Francisco-Oakland, Sacramento, San Jose, Lake Tahoe, and the Monterey Peninsula can never be taken away. Nor can the generally mild and rain-free weather which is the envy of people in humid areas throughout the nation.

The job opportunities that Compaglia, the former county planning commission chairman, pointed to as crucial to the growing up of Contra Costa remain plentiful and more varied than ever.

White-collar employment opportunities will increase with the steady fill-up of futuristic office buildings in the central county. Maturation and transition of the economies in the eastern and western sections of Contra Costa will procure more jobs and take the

pressure—at least some of it—off overburdened thoroughfares.

During the last decade, even in previously industrialized portions of the county, service jobs have been the most readily available source of work. This is a trend certain to continue in the foreseeable future as many new businesses emerge to serve a growing residential population and expanding private sector.

Competition for employment in the county will become increasingly tough, prompting many job hunters to look to the metropolitan areas for opportunities. The Contra Costa economy is impacted by what occurs on a national scope. Yet this region has a proven track record—because of its private-sector

*Above: A mother and her child take a moment to admire colorful autumn leaves in Lafayette. Photo by Bob Rowan/Progressive Image*

*Above, top: The family unit lends a strong base to life in Contra Costa. With two-income households on the rise, the care and education of children is becoming a vital concern. Photo by C. Curtis Corlew II*

*Above: Industrial positions are still an important aspect of the job market in Contra Costa, as illustrated by this worker at the PG&E plant near Martinez. Photo by Bob Rowan/Progressive Image*

*Right: Due to the increase of professional business, combined with an abundance of affordable office space, many Contra Costa residents are now able to work within the county, avoiding a long commute to the San Francisco area. Photo by Bob Rowan/ Progressive Image*

diversity—of withstanding trying times far better than other places, an attribute that will be most important to the county in the years ahead.

Contra Costa has managed to retain enough inherent, positive characteristics to make it attractive to individuals and businesses for a long time to come. Perhaps Lee Walton, who served the cities of Antioch, Pleasant Hill, and Martinez as city manager, has the soundest advice when he says not to believe all the projections for the county offered up from countless directions.

"I remember a bank report a couple of decades ago that gave the east county no chance of ever being a significant population center. But look what's happened. Contra Costa has matured beyond most people's wildest dreams. What happens in the future will largely be dictated by the amount of progress made in solving transportation problems. Nevertheless, you can always expect a little bit of the unexpected. That's what makes living here so interesting."

# CHAPTER 3

*Ultramodern office complexes can be found throughout Contra Costa, some reach into the sky while others sprawl among beautifully landscaped grounds. The town of Walnut Creek features Two Walnut Creek Center, a complex which was designed in a stunning geometric style. Photo by Mark Gibson*

# OFFICE DEVELOPMENT

**S**hould a logo ever be needed to capture the essence of Contra Costa County's economic progress story, there would be little argument over one of its central themes.

If they glanced toward the heavens for inspiration, the "idea people" commissioned to design such a logo could not miss the futuristic office structures that reach to the sky in virtually every portion of the county.

These buildings come in all shapes and sizes and contain "Star Wars" technology which can activate everything from air conditioning to outside water sprinkler systems. The external appearance of these structures and the complexes they form are of award-winning quality.

The many thousands of new county-based workers who have filled these handsome edifices during the last decade and a half are representative of the dramatic shift in the composition of the regional economy. Now, and presumably for years to come, white-collar professions—everything from medicine and accounting to data processing and insurance—will be the principal source of employment in the county. Heavy industry, though still important to the overall job picture, has been permanently relegated to a supporting role in this chronicle of progress.

Transformation of our private sector to one that is primarily service oriented is as rock solid as the concrete which serves as the cornerstones of Contra Costa's office buildings.

The proven attractiveness of all the county as a premier place to live and work is reflected by the glass-adorned business parks that enhance cities like Concord, San Ramon, and Walnut Creek. "Ambience" is the term some magazine writers and demographers use to describe this eternal, endearing asset. Others choose the words "suburban sophistication."

The end result of this maturation process, symbolized by the new wave of office buildings, is a county population that is generally more affluent, educated, and mobile than it was even a decade ago. The many new Contra Costa residents have supplemented the county's private sector and contributed significantly to the overall betterment of the entire Bay Area.

How does one measure prestige? In terms of its application to a geographic area, involvement by major corporations in forging economic prosperity is a critical gauge.

A yearning to reduce their presence in aging, crowded, and expensive Bay Area big cities motivated such corporate giants as Chevron, Bank of America, Pacific Bell, and Wells Fargo Bank to relocate large-scale office operations to Contra Costa. With the well-publicized moves, these companies and others gained an important benefit essential to heightened productivity. Employee morale was given a boost as many employees were given the long-awaited chance to work close to their homes in Contra Costa. Surveys by corporations making the relocations revealed that as many as 50 percent of the transplanted staffers resided in this county.

These titans of American business found anything but a corporate wasteland when they transferred major white-collar divisions here. Long-thriving enterprises like Longs Drugs, CP National, Liquid Air, Jacuzzi, Breuner's Home Furnishings, and Lesher Communications were among the notable pioneers of Contra Costa's private-sector boom. They were the catalysts for the even greater economic expansion of the county fueled by the entry into the office market of major, household-name corporations.

Over the last several years in this county, office parks have become business parks—scenic settings for not only traditional clerical functions but research,

*Facing page, top: The successful Bishop Ranch in San Ramon is representative of the many modern office developments being constructed to house the county's thriving white-collar businesses. Photo by Roc DeWilde*

*Above and left: Service companies and white-collar workers are becoming the foundation of Contra Costa's economy. Photos by Bob Rowan/ Progressive Image*

*Facing page, bottom: Shadelands in Walnut Creek is a stunning example of the numerous landscaped office parks being established in the county. This pleasing complex incorporates graceful settings and provides ample parking as well as a good selection of varying office space for its tenants. Photo by Roc DeWilde*

product development, and manufacturing as well. An exceptional embodiment of such diversity is Shadelands, a well-established park of mostly two- and three-story buildings situated in eastern Walnut Creek. This striking merger of new and not-so-new architectural styles is a good example of the environment that employers and employees find so appealing.

Clustered in this one complex are a wide variety of businesses which provide a livelihood for nearly 10,000 men and women. Free and plentiful parking, recreational facilities, and proximity to entertainment and shopping centers are a few of its selling points.

Insurance giants like The Travelers have set up regional offices there. Food purveyor Del Monte engages in important research projects at its impressive Shadelands laboratories. At the Lesher Communications headquarters, several regional newspapers and the national edition of the *New York Times* are published. High technology is represented by Dow Chemical, Zehntel, and Varian. Chevron, Kaiser Health Plan,

Wells Fargo Bank, and Xerox are among the companies that have tapped Shadelands' expansive office space to handle the paperwork and computer tasks that are part of every big business.

Parks like this one have not thrived at the expense of office complexes located in the downtown sections of other Contra Costa communities. Their emergence has, instead, blessed the region with an impressive array of different business settings, each with its own special appeal. This valuable asset of variety in office environments has given the county a competitive edge in the unceasing effort to lease the many thousands of square feet of new work space annually being created.

A much-ballyhooed attribute of the spacious, statuesque office buildings in downtown Concord and Walnut Creek is their nearness to Bay Area Rapid Transit stations. This is a plus of no small consequence in light of the traffic snarls that characterize the central county's transportation challenge.

Emergence of Shadelands and other business parks into prestigious addresses for offices and other kinds of uses also exemplifies a different, though impor-

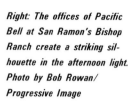

tant, demographic movement. Migration of companies away from the Bay Area's metropolitan areas was largely due to many employers' desire to create a more pleasant setting for their workers—one which would inevitably increase productivity. Placing workers in parks situated on the outskirts of cities near to residential areas fostered the intended upbeat spirit. Many employees had substantially reduced commutes that enabled them to give more time and energy to their workdays.

The role of office developers in improving the county's infrastructure and workers' quality of life cannot be overlooked. For example, Sunset Development—builder of San Ramon's highly successful Bishop Ranch—took a leadership role in bringing about improvements to bustling Freeway 680.

Sunset also arranged and implemented an effective, farsighted transportation plan that included the operation of Bishop Ranch-owned express buses that link the sprawling business park and the Walnut Creek BART station. These buses are not only a plus for the thousands of businessmen and women from such Bishop Ranch tenants as Chevron, Pacific Bell,

and Beckman Instruments; they contribute also to the on-going effort to ease south county traffic, serving as more than just a symbolic gesture toward that goal.

Recognizing the ever-increasing place of women in the county work force, Sunset and other major office developers are at the forefront of the effort to ensure that affordable, quality child care is sufficiently available for this growing region.

The demand for continuing education by all levels of personnel and the companies for whom they work has resulted in learning centers being situated within office complexes. At Bishop Ranch, a joint facility involving several colleges and universities has met with a high level of acceptance. The convenience to employers and employees stemming from such facilities is reason to believe that office-based classrooms are here to stay.

From roughly 1975 to 1985 significant fortunes were amassed by individuals and companies in the business of constructing Contra Costa offices. Not all of them, it should be noted, came from California or even the United States. Canadian and Japanese investors figured prominently in this modern-day rush for suburban gold. Yet just as rapidly as they entered the market, many of these foreigners departed for seemingly greener pastures.

In their place entered well-known insurance companies not the least bit hesitant to bank at least a portion of their future prosperity on the long-term promise of the Contra Costa economy.

As the 1980s neared an end, insurers and retirement funds had become a principal source of funding for new, major commercial projects in Contra Costa.

The proliferation of office space in this county did not happen overnight, although to some people it seemed that way. The high vacancy rates for office space in the county that clouded the region's business outlook entering the 1990s also took a while to develop. Factors that set the stage for heightening of the Contra Costa skyline—i.e., an abundance of relatively affordable, vacant land coupled with dwindling vacancies and escalating rents in San Francisco—remained in place for several years.

Slight cracks in the county's office firmament became evident in the early 1980s, however, as a few significant office users—most notably, Woodward and Clyde environmental consultants—returned to San Francisco from what turned out to be temporary offices in the Concord-Walnut Creek area. The reasons, ironically, were pretty much the same as those spurring their move to Contra Costa, centering around declining rents and increasing office space in the city.

Just about the same time, the seeds were being sown for anti-growth movements in key central county cities, motivated by mounting transportation problems. Although varying in effectiveness and only temporary in the minds of many economists, these no-

growth attitudes raised questions about the long-range direction of the Contra Costa economy.

There was virtually no doubting the important role transportation played in the buildup of the county. Brisk office development took place on and around BART terminal property throughout Contra Costa, including the affluent burgs of Orinda and Lafayette.

The blossoming of both San Ramon and nearby Pleasanton was, it is true, achieved without the benefit of actual BART rail service. The Tri-Valley region, in which both cities are located, overcame that shortcoming by capitalizing on its possession of the convergence of two major freeways (580 and 680). Hilltop, the Richmond area's sprawling, successful business park, similarly profited from its proximity to heavily traveled Interstate 80.

The ability to move tremendous numbers of people created by the combination of major freeway systems and BART rail service has helped establish Concord and Walnut Creek as impressive office centers. The distinctive structures that have gone up in both communities are testimony to the swift road to success that the county has traveled.

Still in the formulative stages is perhaps the most stunning example of BART's role in causing large-scale business development. The hotly contested unincorporated land near the Pleasant Hill BART station sprouted residential and office buildings beginning in the 1970s.

During recent years, the much-vaunted area has taken giant steps toward fulfilling its considerable potential. Catalyst for the buildup was Central Bank, which dur-

ing the early 1980s relocated its administrative headquarters from San Francisco to Treat Boulevard. The stately brick structure has become a symbol of the promise steadily being realized by the Concord-Walnut Creek urban village.

Close to the Central Bank building are stylish mid-rise office buildings designed to house a number of white-collar tenants. Professional offices of one and two stories, specialty shops, and perhaps a hotel will fill out this focal point of new county growth in the near future.

Given the momentous niche that office development has carved in the Contra Costa progress story, it was predictable that industry leaders would be cast in the limelight. A 1987 cover story in *Diablo Magazine* about the richest people of the East Bay included, very notably, Albert D. Seeno, Sr., Peter Bedford, and Alex Mehran—all key players in the county's office building scenario.

Almost as quickly as Walnut Creek established a reputation as the financial hub of the county, the same city became a center for companies involved in office development and/or leasing.

While large owner/tenant complexes like those filled by Bank of America and Chevron in Concord grab the headlines, it is speculative office space that has comprised the bulk of new commercial construction in Contra Costa during the past 15 years.

Speculative office building has become a buzz-word of the county private sector, and rightly so. There is more than a small measure of charisma and dar-

ing attached to people who put up buildings without the luxury and revenue of a single pre-signed tenant. In the actions of these developers is embodied the ultimate confidence in the Contra Costa economy.

There is no doubt that the speculative office market is highly risky. Its history is dotted with stories of success and failure. Into which category a developer falls hinges largely on the breadth and depth of his financial resources.

For the most part, these are very wise and wealthy individuals who engage in speculative construction. They research an area well before breaking the first shovelful of ground. Wisely, they enlist the services of leasing agents with extensive knowledge of the region.

Location has proven to be the name of the game when it comes to erecting speculative office structures. Veteran developers like Albert Seeno, Sr., Ernie Graham, Jon Reynolds, and David Brown have been astute in placing their complexes on sites with significant potential for success.

Take the case of Reynolds and Brown, prominent builders of industrial and office space in southern Alameda County. Well before Pacific Southwest Airways made its decision in early 1986 to start service between Concord's Buchanan Field and Los Angeles International Airport, the two developers were mapping major development plans for the area across from the Sheraton Hotel and Business Center.

What they carved out along well-trafficked Concord Avenue was a magnificent complex named, appropriately, Airport Plaza. Helped tremendously by the agree-

ment of Wells Fargo Bank to situate its credit card accounting operation in one full phase of the project, Reynolds and Brown quickly had a winner on their hands.

Proximity to Buchanan Field—like closeness to BART—will turn out to be a valuable asset in the future, most regional economists contend. The promise of additional commercial service in and out of the busy airport has steadily lured companies to offices within close range of Buchanan. Continuation of this trend appears assured in the future.

The brisk business in office construction that began in the central county during the mid-1970s, symbolized by the 10-story Fidelity building in downtown

Walnut Creek, followed a somewhat predictable, geographic pattern. From Contra Costa's core—i.e., the Concord-Walnut Creek urban village—office development spread rather rapidly to other portions of the county.

Cities such as Antioch and Martinez, boosted by a proliferation of reasonably priced residences in their midst, learned the positive meaning of commercial development spillover. As land quickly was eaten up in central Contra Costa, developers focused their attention in these other directions.

Highway 4, stretching from Pinole to Stockton, generated more than subtle glances from office builders. Though not the rival of Freeways 580 and 680 in terms of vehicular traffic, "4" still piqued significant developer interest.

The relatively affordable housing blossoming along that route was a catalyst for many good things to happen. Areawide shopping centers with name, anchor tenants sprang up in places like Pinole, Martinez, Antioch, and Oakley. Educational and medical facilities were expanded and improved to service the growing population. And slowly but surely, transportation remedies were funded by a combination of local, state, and federal agencies.

Large-scale commercial building activity occurring in communities like Walnut Creek, Concord, Richmond, and San Ramon served as a springboard for business and residential growth countywide.

This growth withstood the tests of national and regional business doldrums and forged very distinctive office markets that, taken together, made Contra Costa so appealing to a wide spectrum of developers.

Handsome high-technology complexes, hotels, and professional offices have combined with Victorian-style residences to provide Martinez with both new life and a new look. Helping fuel this commercial development has been the surge of new home building in the newer portions of the city close to Lafayette and Pleasant Hill.

A home rush also unfolded, beginning in the early 1970s, on the segment of "4" from west Pittsburg all the way east to Discovery Bay in Byron where a recreational and residential community emerged on former marshland. Provision of homes in a wide range of prices helped create a divergent population in the east county. In a relatively short period, the Antioch-Pittsburg area shook off its domination by heavy industry and assumed a generally white-collar economy.

Major changes enveloping the private sectors of east and west Contra Costa during the 1980s mirrored the trend happening countywide.

The Association of Bay Area Governments, a nonprofit regional agency that monitors growth and its resultant effects on the quality of life, has projected that service jobs will be the most important source of new

*Above: Airport Plaza is strategically located along Concord Avenue near Buchanan Field. Photo by Roc DeWilde*

*Right: Even high-tech medical offices, like the Mount Diablo Hospital complex in Concord, are appearing across the county in an effort to serve the growing needs of the population. Photo by Roc De-Wilde*

employment in the county through the first decade of
the twenty-first century and beyond.

By the year 2000, ABAG economists predict that
the service category will account for a total of
125,000 full- and part-time jobs in Contra Costa. The association notes that many of the new positions will
result from a growing demand for office-related activities such as accounting, temporary help, legal and
other professional consulting, and computer programming. All of these service providers, save for the very
small minority who work out of their homes, require
office space.

A recent phenomenon of the Contra Costa business scene is the wave of previously nontraditional shopping center tenants who have set up offices in retail settings. Among supermarkets and drugstores can now
be found the offices of dentists, radio stations, and
even pet clinics.

Ongoing definition of what will prove to be the long-
term make up of the Contra Costa office sector has
critical implications for all who live and work in the
county. Among the major questions posed in the
1985 Growth Trends report of the Contra Costa Community Development Department were:

—What will be the effect upon the county's economy of a surplus of office space and high vacancy
rates due to overbuilding?

—How will the new office jobs that are created
affect Contra Costa's cultural and social characteristics?

—How will the large number of industrial and
office jobs planned for the Livermore-Amador Valley
in southern Alameda County impact Contra Costa
and, more specifically, the San Ramon Valley?

The softening of the county office sector during
the latter part of the 1980s delayed confrontation, to
some degree, with those last two questions.

Oft-quoted authorities on office building and leasing in the East Bay generally agree that a fresh
resurgence of such activity is not far down the road.

According to Jeffrey S. Weil, senior marketing con-
sultant for the Grubb & Ellis Company, the factor
most responsible for the dropoff in office absorption
along the Interstate 680 Corridor was the overbuilt
San Francisco market. As the 1990s materialized,
Weil and others in his industry forecasted a significant tightening of available office space in the city.

The result, Weil feels, is certain rental rate escala-
tions in San Francisco, prompting corporations to flee
to the East Bay with the same kind of flourish that
was the case in the early 1980s.

Weil is confident of renewed I-680 growth, basing his prediction on four key factors: the region's excellent executive labor pool; long-range, brisk residential
growth in east Contra Costa, Solano, southern
Alameda, Stockton, Tracy, and Manteca—all areas
within relatively reasonable commuting distance of established office centers in this county; the generally pro-

*Above: The need for office sup-
port activities, such as data entry, computer programming, se-
cretarial, and legal services are
expected to increase in the coming years. Photo by Bob Rowan/
Progressive Image*

*Left: The Contra Costa County
Finance Building in Martinez
maintains a strong traditional
style amidst the other modern office structures of the area.
Photo by Mark Gibson*

*Facing page, top: The Station
Plaza office building, owned
by Thomas Properties, makes
a bold architectural statement.
Photo by Bob Rowan/
Progressive Image*

*Facing page, center: The old
and new blend together in
many of Contra Costa's communities, as seen here in Walnut
Creek, since more and more
land is being developed for
much-needed office space.
Photo by Roc DeWilde*

*Facing page, bottom: The inter-
play between glass and light cre-
ates spectacular imagery on
the many glass-adorned office
structures in Contra Costa.
Photo by Bob Rowan/
Progressive Image*

business position held by local governments in the region; and the substantial amount of undeveloped or underutilized office sites available for development, as especially evidenced in San Ramon, the Pleasant Hill BART station area, and Concord.

The trying times that some office builders and leasing agents in Contra Costa had to endure in the 1980s was predictable. So, too, was the turnaround which began to take seed with the dawning of the new decade.

"There's reason to be optimistic. The 1990s will be like a rubber band snapping forward when it comes to the rejuvenation of the county office market," said Ed Del Becarro, a veteran of the commercial leasing industry in Contra Costa. "There will be no big chunks of developable office space left in the county by 1992."

Heightened appreciation of residential values in the central county will prompt a migration of some previously Concord- and Walnut Creek-based office operations to east Contra Costa and Solano, Del Becarro believes. "Walnut Creek will become almost solely a setting for high-end tenants. Concord will be primarily midrises. San Ramon will continue to draw a variety of office users."

Further equalization of labor costs between Contra Costa and the San Francisco-Oakland metropolitan area will not negatively affect Contra Costa, according to Del Becarro.

"The county's labor force has assumed added sophistication and stature in recent years. That works in its favor in the eyes of corporate decision-makers," Del Becarro contends.

Pacific Gas & Electric, in its East Bay Economic Forecast compiled for 1987, underscored the changing nature of the region's private sector and the resultant impact on the Contra Costa office market.

"Our outlook for non-durable manufacturing employment growth in the East Bay is about one-half percent per year through 1990. By comparison, finance and service industries will be growing about 5 percent per year," predicted the PG&E economists.

FIRE, that striking abbreviation for the combination of financial, insurance, and real estate businesses, will ignite a new era of brisk office construction and leasing activity in Contra Costa.

Growth management measures planned for San Francisco are expected by several regional forecasters to play a significant role in forging a new era of economic prosperity for this county. The incentives being offered by developers to potential lessees, though short-lived, will also contribute to the revival.

The shakeout of Contra Costa's office sector that occurred in the late 1980s came as no great surprise to people in the know. The same can and will be said of the coming resurgence—a progress story sure to touch every corner of this county.

# CHAPTER 4

The dreams and vitality of Contra Costans, from the early settlers to the present-day entrepreneurs, have created a vibrant sense of community and industry in the county. These energetic runners burst forth at the start of the Walnut Festival 10K Run, one of the oldest continuously running events in the state. Photo by Bob Rowan/ Progressive Image

# "NAME PLAYERS" AND VISIONS

The advancement of Contra Costa County into new business frontiers and eras of prosperity has been a story, first and foremost, of people who have given of their energy and skills to see the region's dreams fulfilled.

To parks, schools, streets, and even cities have been applied the names of early pioneers who first shaped life here and set the stage for future progress. Save for history buffs, their contributions are lost on virtually all the county's present-day residents.

But that is a fact of life. Leaders die and new ones take up their mantle. Fortunate are we to have around us individuals who observed and guided the magnificent maturation of Contra Costa. Unbelievable, yet true: the near-total transformation of the county's economy was accomplished in roughly three decades—from 1955 to 1985.

In our midst are many people who noticed the area's potential for greatness well before it was detected by the rest of the outside world. "Visionary" is not a title easily earned. Nonetheless, it is a fitting designation for several people from business and other corners of society who have helped make Contra Costa one of the most dynamic counties in America.

The occupations represented by these farsighted folks run the gamut and mirror the diversity of the region. Some visionaries were born here. Others brought to the county the lessons of success learned in other places. They share an enthusiasm for the many attributes of Contra Costa and a willingness to solve the challenges that inevitably stem from "bigness."

Dean S. Lesher, more than 85-years-young and one of the county's most vocal cheerleaders, has at least one newspaper in every geographic section of Contra Costa. The one-time Kansas City trial lawyer got his first view of this portion of the East Bay while on an aerial tour in 1947. "It was obvious how beautiful Contra Costa was and how it possessed the potential for expansion," said the publisher who, shortly after that flight, purchased the twice-weekly *Courier-Journal*, forerunner to the *Contra Costa Times*.

Lesher has been a strong supporter of economic diversity and a quality of life that is enhanced, not damaged, by business and residential growth. The Harvard-educated entrepreneur and his wife, Margaret, have headed efforts to expand and improve educational, health, and recreational facilities. In the latter part of the 1980s, the couple focused their efforts on three goals: increased adult literacy in the county; development of a regional arts center in Walnut Creek; and construction of a state university satellite campus near the Concord-Clayton border.

Education has been the center of the newspaper baron's attention since he settled in the county more than four decades ago. "The strength of our schools has been a big asset in attracting new business to the area. We are blessed with outstanding private colleges and universities and a first-class community college system. A state university would complement these institutions we already have in place."

With his newspaper empire now branching through much of the Bay Area and numbering in excess of 35 publications, Lesher is well aware that no county is an island when it comes to crucial infrastructure concerns. As president of the Contra Costa Council (formerly the Development Association) in the mid-1980s, immediately following the organization's separation from public funding, he spearheaded an effort to ensure that the county's housing, educational, and sewage facilities kept pace with population increases. Through a well-devised network of task forces comprised of persons considered authorities in their fields, the council was able to thoroughly confront the critical issues facing the region.

Two other notable achievements of Lesher's council presidency were his ability to attract top corporate leaders to active participation in the group, and the expansion of the membership to include a wide range of county businesses. The council encouraged dialogue between the private and public sectors which proved valuable in helping reach solutions to a wide range of challenges. Lesher's effectiveness and magnetism in getting others involved in problem solving was undisputable.

A visionary is able to perceive the possibility for achievement and then make it happen. When it comes to the newspaper business, Lesher has demonstrated that ability in stunning fashion.

The *Contra Costa Times*, flagship of the sprawling group, has shaken the status of a shopping paper and improved to the point where it has captured the respect of publishers of Bay Area metros. Lesher dailies in Pinole, Antioch, and Pleasanton have taken advantage of the rapid growth in their areas to raise circulation and advertising revenues. Never one to lose sight

*Facing page, top: Martinez residents are proud of their heritage and historic marina. Crafts of all sizes make this charming marina their home. Photo by Roc DeWilde*

*Below: Publisher Dean S. Lesher, an active and prominent citizen in the county, supports the enhancement of life through commercial and residential growth. The main facility of his newspaper, the* Contra Costa Times, *is located at the Shadelands office park in Walnut Creek. Photo by Bob Rowan/Progressive Image*

*Bob Hilson, Sr., of Hilson's Family Apparel adjusts his trademark bow tie at his Martinez store. Photo by Roc DeWilde*

of the community aspect of suburban journalism, the astute publisher has maintained weekly publications in Concord, Danville, and Lafayette.

"It is our job to report on the progress happening in all the places we serve," said Lesher. "Our employees are involved in numerous organizations which help promote the public good. We feel we have helped bring about change for the better in many situations."

During his many years in the county, Lesher has learned the inherent differences between cities and geographical areas. "They all bring strength and vitality to the larger picture," he said. "Interaction between communities has increased because of the urgency to confront pressing issues like transportation and housing. Progress is being made because of a cooperative spirit and recognition of the great stakes that are involved."

The influx of thousands of new people to the county has very much changed the nature of cities, Lesher noted. "We are seeing more and more commuting within Contra Costa. The result is two different kinds of local populations: residents and workers. Each has shown the willingness to become involved in activities that make for a better quality of life."

In the shining constellation that is the county economy, small- and medium-size businesses have be-

come vivid stars. These retail and service providers have generally flourished because of hard work, wise budgeting, and genuine concern for the customer. One individual who has what it takes is Bob Hilson, Sr.

From his tiny second-story office on Main Street in Martinez, Hilson seems to savor reminiscing about the early days of the county's development. "For a good part of this century, this city was the retailing center of the region. We had almost all the major retail stores. The big increase of population in Concord and Walnut Creek changed that and left Martinez with pretty much just city government for a number of years. This city is making a comeback. Improvement of the downtown, the marina, and the entire waterfront area has helped immensely."

The sale of family apparel has been the Hilson family business for most of this century. Through good and not-so-good times, the enterprise has succeeded by establishing a base of loyal customers. With numerous discount retailers entering the Contra Costa marketplace during the last several decades, the Hilsons have heightened their emphasis on personal service.

From the front of his Martinez store, first opened in 1912, Hilson can hear the sounds of train whistles

and ship horns. They spark a monologue about an era when the county was very different from the one we know now. "Main Street was basically a dirt trail when we started out here. People traveled by horse and buggy to do their shopping.

"Our employees used to go down to the docks to pick up goods for the store off the ships," Hilson recalled. "Transportation has been a major factor in the county's expansion and maturation. Our society has become much more mobile. Many people drive from one end of the area to the other every day to go to work. You didn't see that in the old days."

The advances in people-moving that have unfolded in Contra Costa in the last two decades astound Hilson and others who have long resided in the region. "BART contributed heavily to the economic growth of the county, no doubt about it. Development of the airport [Buchanan Field] so it can accommodate scheduled service by major carriers is a big plus. I know that many businesses are using those flights between here and Los Angeles. When all the planned freeway work is completed, there will probably be a new wave of expansion."

When it comes to identifying *the* major factor in Contra Costa's maturation, Hilson doesn't have to grope for an answer. "Affordable housing was the principal reason we grew as fast as we did. In relative terms, compared to the rest of the Bay Area, the county is still more affordable when it comes to buying or renting a house.

"Major corporations have been attracted to the county because of the factors of affordable housing for their employees and reasonable costs for land and office rentals. In Martinez, as an example, there have been many new homes built during the last few years on the other side of Highway 4, toward Lafayette. Their affordability has contributed to the construction of many new businesses along the freeway through this city," Hilson said.

The expansion of Hilson's Family Apparel to new locations in Concord, Antioch, and Benicia mirrored the business build-out of the region. It also demonstrated that small-and medium-size firms, if efficiently managed and properly situated, could benefit from Contra Costa's blossoming as an elite economic entity.

Not all of the pacesetters and pioneers of the county's private sector were home grown. A case in point is Longs Drugs, a splendid retailing success story which began in Oakland in 1938.

Sons of a Mendocino County general store proprietor, the chain's founders—Joseph and Thomas Long—swung open the doors of their first store on Piedmont Avenue that year. The $25,000 loan needed for

*Transportation has played a major role in the expansion of Contra Costa by providing ease of movement for businesses and residents. The 680-24 interchange is probably the busiest section of freeway in the East Bay area. Photo by Bob Rowan/ Progressive Image*

start-up of the Oakland business proved a very prudent investment.

Since its founding a half-century ago, Longs has been transformed from a traditional drugstore operation to a general merchandiser which offers its millions of customers everything from food items to fishing gear to electrical appliances to cosmetics. The company's performance on the New York Stock Exchange has been very rewarding to Longs' shareholders and a source of encouragement to those county residents toying with the thought of starting their own business.

The steady growth of Longs from the days of that humble beginning on Piedmont Avenue is nothing short of meteoric. Now numbering more than 220 stores in the West and Hawaii, the chain has adeptly pursued a course of movement into areas with strong potential for future major development.

Establishment in 1970 of its corporate headquarters on Civic Drive in Walnut Creek showed clearly

*Longs Drug Stores corporation, the headquarters of which are located on Civic Drive in Walnut Creek, embodies a spirit of competitive industry and concern for community issues and concerns. Photo by Bob Rowan/ Progressive Image*

the esteem Longs Drugs held for Contra Costa. That decision provided the county with the prestigious, marquee kind of business name that would be a magnet for other well-known corporations.

The Walnut Creek that the Longs relocated to from Oakland was far different from the Walnut Creek of today—a city crisscrossed by BART tracks and dotted by mid-rise office structures. Enticed here by the space available in the county and the steps being taken to enhance the quality of life, the Long brothers have strongly reaffirmed their position that this is a great place to do business.

Since setting up headquarters in the geographic center of Contra Costa, Longs has opened stores in virtually every portion of the county. Two decades after they took the bold step of basing their growing company in the Walnut Creek area, Tom and Joseph Long point out with unmistakable pride to the many other firms of nationwide stature that have done the same. Those include Liquid Air and CP National, both located in downtown Walnut Creek; Western Temporary Services, Zehntel, and Lesher Communications in Shadelands; and Central Bank, near the Pleasant Hill BART station.

Both residents of Contra Costa (Tom lives in Alamo and Joseph in Danville), the Longs have quietly and without fanfare given their support and financial resources to numerous county causes through foundations bearing their names.

The well-used axiom about "giving something back" to the community from whence one has drawn a living has been exemplified by many of the county's visionaries—Lesher, Hilson, and the Long brothers among them.

Although their styles of contribution have differed widely, futuristic-thinking individuals have improved the quality of life for all who call Contra Costa home. The realms of athletics and the arts have been upgraded by the good deeds of these people of vision. In addition, colleges, hospitals, and public service agencies have been able to realize their goals because of assistance from local leaders.

Were it not for the activism and funding put forth by caring people, the county today might not have such facilities as the three community colleges, the Concord Pavilion, the East Bay Regional Parks, and Walnut Creek Civic Theater.

In its relatively short modern era, the county has added critical infrastructure that counterparts in other areas of the nation took double the time—or more— to develop. The term "public-private partnership" is frequently misstated or misused. There is no denying, however, that it has had an important role in making Contra Costa a better place to live and work.

Representatives of business and government have cooperated to forge answers to such haunting questions as those involving housing, transportation, and

*Left: This audience enjoyed a summertime picnic while attending the 1988 Concord Jazz Festival at the Concord Pavilion. Photo by Roc DeWilde*

*Facing page, top: Situated across the bay from San Francisco, Richmond has been mostly dependent on heavy industry for its economic strength. Recently, however, several new enterprises have begun to change the city's future by bringing in new corporations, research and development, and real estate speculation. Photo by Mark Gibson*

*Below: Young and old alike take pleasure in the many biking trails featured at Contra Loma Regional Park in Antioch. Photo by Meri Simon*

education. Start-up in the mid-1980s of bus systems serving virtually all of the county could be traced directly to the joint effort of the private and public sectors to relieve the congestion on area roads.

People have come from far and near to help Contra Costa achieve greatness. Longstanding businesses, many of them passed down by families through succeeding generations, have proved a source of emulation and stability for a county almost always enveloped in change.

"I've seen it over and over again in the west county. We have plenty of second- and third-generation businesses. It's kind of like 'Sons of the Pioneers,'" mused Jack Horton, retired executive vice president of the Richmond Chamber of Commerce.

"The people who head these firms give much-needed continuity to the area. They bridge the different stages in the development of our city. The family connection gives them the ability to put a historical perspective on the challenges we currently face," said Horton, a resident of Richmond for more than 50 years.

Well-established enterprises like Mechanics Bank in Richmond and Bio-Rad in nearby Hercules have been models for later occupants of the west county to follow, Horton said. "The progress made by this area has been attributable to the efforts of companies, large and small, old and new, and to the hard work of people, rich and poor."

Richmond, for a long time almost solely dependent on heavy industry for economic survival, has blended the old with the new as well as any community in Contra Costa. Horton and others are convinced that the city's ability to carve a new future for itself is the product of numerous visions being successfully melded together.

"There is a unity here, a singleness of spirit that makes things happen," remarked the 35-year veteran of Richmond's chamber. "The old-timers have teamed with new residents to create a strategy that has given the city vitality."

The rebounding of Richmond has been tied in large part to the vision of its leading employer, the San Francisco-based Chevron Company. The huge refinery that the oil giant has expanded and improved over the last several decades has been a model for its competitors to pattern.

Success of the reigning complex has served as the springboard for Chevron to play a leading role in the turnaround of the aging city. Location of the company's Ortho garden products division not far from the refinery provided Richmond with a research and development enterprise that would inspire other kinds of technological firms to settle in the west county's biggest municipality.

Possibly the most instrumental force in the molding of a new Richmond has been Chevron Land, the real estate arm of the huge corporation. Hilltop, the 900-plus-acre diversified development overlooking busy Interstate 80, has blossomed under the careful leadership and orchestration of the oil company subsidiary. A regional shopping mall, offices, research and development facilities, and an auto park

*Below: The Chevron Refinery, located on Richmond's waterfront, continues to be the economic mainstay of West Contra Costa County. Photo by Jordan Coonrad*

have given the former industrial property a near-complete facelift.

The role of corporations as visionaries and stylists of a brighter future has been substantial, Horton and others believe. "These companies have backed up their desire to bring about better communities with actions that have enhanced the quality of life. The city is making progress because Chevron and other firms are lending their talent and resources to filling the needs of the city."

In Richmond's case, the combination of demographic and geographic assets has served as the basis for well-planned expansion. Solution of nagging transportation problems through the creation of new freeways puts the community in position to fully achieve its considerable potential for greatness.

Jerry Fitzpatrick, Sr., was selling Chevrolets in Concord when there was no Bank of America center, no Sunvalley shopping mall, no major hotels, and no midrise office buildings.

His dealership on Diamond Boulevard is situated near Chevron's national travel card complex, the Hilton Hotel, Willows Shopping Center, and the burgeoning Airport Plaza development across from Buchanan Field.

"Things have really, really changed," noted Fitzpatrick. "I remember when this city was filled with orchards and lots of places to go duck hunting. Fortunately we have retained considerable recreational space. The businesses that have come in here have contributed tremendously to a higher quality of life for all of us. Companies are people; we can't forget that. Employees of many of these firms have become involved in government and community activities. The growing up of Contra Costa has been accomplished because of a fine blending of the old, the new, and the middle."

In becoming the county's most populous city, Concord—in Fitzpatrick's eyes—has not lost the small-town qualities so many people enjoy. "We still have the parades, the festivals, and the clubs and other groups that were with us when the city was only a shadow of its current self. I hope they continue on the scene. They are part of the fiber of the community.

"Climate, the intrinsic beauty of the area, and relatively reasonable housing and land costs were key factors in the growth of the county," observed Fitzpatrick. "Those same ingredients are with us today. It should be obvious that the full story of Contra Costa has not been written."

In the thinking of several esteemed demographers and economists, Antioch is destined to become the county's second-largest city (after Concord) before the end of the century. Approaching the 1990s, the Delta community's population stood at 55,000 and rising fast.

Worth Shaw has spent virtually all of his life in Antioch and served the city for more than 30 years as Leisure Services director. Over time he assimilated a myriad of dreams and visions for the riverfront burg. What has materialized, he says, is a patchwork of different people's ideas of what the Antioch of the future should be like.

*Above: Though bustling with activity and growth, Concord still maintains a strong sense of community with an emphasis on local events, clubs, and festivals. Salvio Pacheco Square is a delightful and charming enhancement to this exciting community. Photo by Bob Rowan/Progressive Image*

*Left: Although seemingly still untouched by much progress and development, the Delta community of Antioch is projected to be the second largest city in Contra Costa by the end of the century. Photo by Mark Gibson*

*Far left: The Pacheco Adobe in Concord is an educational and delightful reminder of the county's historical past. Photo by Mark Gibson*

"The visions change with the generations and the size of the town," Shaw said. "But the essence of communities never really changes that much. Antioch—even with all the development—still has a lot of small-town flavor. Not many people anticipated the county would sprout as fast as it has. A city like this one with rapid residential growth has had to anticipate the needs of a growing population. With Leisure Services, like everything else, we've had to expand our offerings accordingly and in the process do some experimenting. Quality of life is a big part of what brought all these new residents and businesses to the county. We can't afford to lose that advantage."

The Tri-Valley, which saddles the Contra Costa-Alameda border near San Ramon, was built up overnight—or, at least, it seemed that way to many observers. "The opening of Freeway 680 early in the 1960s was the catalyst," said John May, longtime shoe-store owner in Danville and the town's first mayor.

"The big wave of home building began immediately after the freeway went in. It was like letting up a window shade to progress. We will never be the same again.

"Climate and environment is a lot of the reason for the development of the region," May continued. "Fortunately, we've been able to hold on to much of the rural atmosphere that made this area so appealing in the first place. Depending where you are in the valley, communities are oriented either toward Walnut Creek or San Jose. There are plenty of our residents who work in both places. Our horizons have shifted, but that could be expected."

To the visionaries we owe a great debt.

Their dedication and hard work in making the county more successful will be rewarded in the years ahead. Succeeding generations will be touched by these individuals. How lucky Contra Costa has been to have them.

# CHAPTER 5

*A BART train makes its way down Highway 24 towards the Walnut Creek station as evening commuters head home after the day's work. Photo by Roc DeWilde*

# TRANSPORTATION: A COMPLEX PUZZLE

**B**e not surprised that transportation-related issues dominate this volume. They have become the hottest topic of conversation among elected officials, business leaders, and the general public in Contra Costa County during the last two decades.

The evolution of this region into one of the most prosperous and vibrant in the state has brought with it increased vehicular traffic and fresh challenges in the realm of mass transit.

The blossoming of the county as a premier address occurred virtually overnight. A blockbuster combination of demographic and economic forces quickly created new commute patterns, overburdening thoroughfares never designed for heavy use.

Transportation problems were an inevitable growing pain for Contra Costa as it became—in the 1970s—one of the fastest-developing counties in America. Although the pace of the region's maturation caught even some veteran Bay Area observers off guard, private and public leaders in the county have displayed a great eagerness to make up for lost time in solving a wide range of challenges to make people-moving trouble free.

It is no surprise that the great public debate over what to do about traffic extended to the political arena in a variety of forms. Slow-growth measures appeared on the ballots of several county communities during the 1980s as very vocal citizen groups tried in their own way to do something about ever-mounting traffic backups. The difference in voter responses to such propositions was clear evidence that the people had their own opinions about what was behind the slow-moving traffic, and how to remedy it.

Candidates in city council and county supervisor races latched on to transportation issues, offering what they billed as fresh perspectives and solutions which would contribute to better traffic flow on area roads. As was the case with the slow-growth measures, voters gave mixed receptions to such candidates.

Hampered by cuts in federal and state funding for transportation improvements, elected officials looked to the private sector and the citizenry as a whole for support in solving transportation difficulties. Developers of sprawling, new office complexes helped fund improvements to freeways which had to carry workers to a myriad of destinations in and outside Contra Costa.

Moves to finance road widening and the like by general tax increases inspired emotional debate among all quarters of county society. A bid to implement that kind of specially earmarked tax successfully qualified for the county ballot in the late 1980s. It went down to defeat, to the anguish of numerous prominent county businessmen who labored long and hard for its approval.

A "we're all in this together" philosophy spawned a cooperative spirit toward fixing nagging transportation problems. Unity unfolded on both a countywide and areawide level. Perhaps the most bizarre example of this happened in east Contra Costa.

Tired of waiting for Bay Area Rapid Transit service to their cities, representatives of Pittsburg, Antioch, and Brentwood made loud, well-publicized overtones about seceding from Contra Costa and forming a new Delta County in which they would not be taxed by BART. The idea was dismissed by many people as unthinkable. It did, however, succeed in demonstrating the east county's anger over not receiving the actual rail service it had been paying for with tax monies for more than 10 years.

Unhappiness with BART took on a countywide complexion during the same time frame in the late 1980s. Preliminary approval by the BART Board to extend service to Colma in San Mateo County—previously a nonmember of the district—raised the hackles of Contra Costa supervisors. The threat of secession was offered in this scenario also, with then-county supervisors chairman Sunne McPeak indicating such a course might be explored if BART did not first serve long-waiting communities in Contra Costa.

McPeak and others were hopeful that the negative situation could be transformed into a positive one, with San Mateo agreeing to subsidize a portion of the cost of bringing BART trains to east Contra Costa.

Frayed tempers come with waiting in a sea of traffic or killing time until the next BART train arrives. The arrival of the commuter age in Contra Costa brought some interesting side effects.

Cellular car phones became fixtures in the autos of many county business executives, affording them

*Below: Though many improvements have been made to local freeways and roads throughout the county, the issue of solving the problem for funding future improvements continues to be a heated concern. Photo by Roc DeWilde*

*Facing page, top: Bay Area Rapid Transit provides an effective transportation alternative for the increasing number of daily commuters in Contra Costa. Photo by Bob Rowan/ Progressive Image*

*Facing page, bottom: Commuters on their way home from San Francisco patiently wait in an evening queue at the west entrance of the Caldecott Tunnel. Photo by Roc DeWilde*

the chance to handle office transactions while being stalled in traffic at the 680-24 junction or other busy intersections. Radio station traffic reports attracted a high level of listeners; the helicopter pilots furnishing such information became personalities in their own right. Medical-care providers began to offer advice on how to minimize the stress caused by being caught up in traffic.

The City of Concord stretched its residents' imaginations by asking them to describe their "dream commutes." The contest, advertised by huge banners placed strategically on the median strips of high-traffic city streets, drew a large number of entrants. Among their "dream commutes" were double tandem bicycles; a hot-air balloon piloted by Loni Anderson; and a large conveyor belt complete with a dining table, chairs, and lavish breakfast.

One answer to Contra Costa's transportation dilemmas would require residents to earn their living within a 15-minute walk or ride from their homes. But neither Contra Costa nor any other major suburban county in this nation works that way.

For now and well into the future, a significant portion of the county's population will commute to work in the cities of San Francisco, Oakland, and San Jose. With the increased use of car and van pools and buses, and renewed patronage of BART, this segment of the labor force should be accommodated rea-

Above: The 680-24 interchange near Walnut Creek and Lafayette is the busiest section of Contra Costa's freeway system. Photo by Bob Rowan/Progressive Image

Left: The elevated BART route in Walnut Creek runs by Walnut Square. Photo by Roc DeWilde

sonably well in its effort to get to and from the workplace.

The buildup of the county's private sector and establishment of a bona fide reverse commute from other areas in this direction has created added pressure on the county's road system and bus lines.

Somewhat overlooked until fairly recently, the movement of residents within the county has swelled in direct proportion to population increases and the expansion of job opportunities. Antioch residents work in Concord; San Ramon residents, in Walnut Creek; Martinez residents, in Richmond; and so on and so forth.

Contra Costa employers have tried to be understanding about their workers' increasing trials in getting to and from work. Flex time, four-day workweeks, and staggered starting and stopping times have helped ease traffic on county roads.

Yet all of the above components of Contra Costa's transportation puzzle represent only a part of the challenge. There are those who theorize that if Contra Costa possessed a private sector half or less the size of what it is now, there would still be major transportation obstacles for the county to hurdle. They surmise that the geographic location of Contra Costa, being central to the rest of Northern California, makes it inevitable that there will always be great numbers of vehicles traveling through the county en route to other destinations.

There appears to be considerable truth to this line of thinking. A case in point is the George Miller Sr. Bridge which spans the Carquinez Straits between Benicia and Martinez. At the start of holiday weekends and even on regular business commute days, traffic seeking to cross the bridge northbound is frequently backed up all the way into Concord. Unquestionably, many—or maybe even most—of these vehicles are driven by people from places other than Contra Costa County.

The attraction of relatively affordable housing has driven up the population of Solano County by leaps and bounds. What this means for Contra Costa is additional cars on Freeway 680 bound for Benicia Bridge. Attention to a development like this—though not generated from within this county—is essential to the Contra Costa planning process.

Taken together, all the factors behind the heightened traffic on county freeways and byways have given a special urgency to making things better for the hundreds of thousands of people who travel in and through Contra Costa.

Ensuing paragraphs in this chapter will show that, indeed, progress is being made in several crucial areas of the county's transportation challenge. Ongoing success in finding solutions to these many longstanding problems is the result of teamwork by government, business, and community leaders.

Awareness of what ails the county in terms of people-moving has given way to the next stages of the scenario: identifying funding resources and then actually putting remedies in place.

Correcting such momentous bottlenecks as the 680-24 freeway interchange or Benicia Bridge is an arduous, time-consuming process with many hurdles. The stakes in the effort are too high, however, not to do everything to bring these much-needed improvements to fruition. For Contra Costa to remain a splendid place to live and work, there is no alternative but to make these changes.

The theory that there is strength in numbers has motivated county residents to organize groups in order to try and solve very specific transportation problems.

BART extension committees have been prevalent in east Contra Costa for many years. During the late 1980s these very active and visible proponents of rail service to Pittsburg, Antioch, and beyond watched a new campaign take hold of their region. A Highway 4 Task Force was formed to exert extra pressure in the attempt to prod government agencies to at least partially fund the widening of that busy freeway.

Martinez, the county seat, has for decades had an understandable but unnerving parking shortage Monday through Friday. To help make things better in that regard, a city parking commission was established. And focusing its attention on traffic bottlenecks in the greater Richmond area has been the West County Transportation Advisory Committee.

The desire to have local control of parking, traffic, and other related challenges played a key role in the successful incorporation drives in Danville and San Ramon.

County government, confronted near the conclusion of the 1980s with the need to formulate a new general plan, thrust its Community Development Department head-first into the effort to assist local jurisdictions in finding ways to alleviate transportation difficulties. A Transportation Planning Division of that office effectively served as a clearinghouse of information and suggestions on people-moving issues in all parts of Contra Costa.

TSM, short for Transportation Systems Management, has become a widely used abbreviation by those in public and private life clamoring for solutions to traffic-caused inconvenience. TSM ordinances predictably surfaced in the central county cities of Concord and Walnut Creek, where vehicular congestion created the heaviest news coverage and public backlash.

A draft TSM ordinance, approved in concept by the Walnut Creek City Council in 1987, called for city employers with 10 or more full-time workers, or employers located in a complex with at least 10 employees, to initiate transportation management steps.

The lengthy approval process for such laws as proposed in Concord and Walnut Creek was set up to

allow for extensive input of residents and businesses regarding transportation problems.

Emergence of a Contra Costa Transportation Partnership Commission, comprised of elected officials from throughout the county, underscored the cooperative approach to fixing regional traffic nuisances. The charge of the commission—according to county Transportation Director Barbara Neustadter—is to map a transportation plan for all of Contra Costa.

"Cities have learned they can no longer operate by themselves in trying to alleviate the traffic snarls that affect all of them to one degree or another. There's little room for provincialism when it comes to the transportation challenge enveloping the county," Neustadter said.

The cooperative approach to molding the future is especially evident in the arena of planning as Contra Costa prepares for the 1990s. Regional planning groups have been formed within the county to make in-depth analyses of the impact of additional growth on such critical areas as housing, waste disposal, educational facilities, and, of course, transportation.

Emanating from such extensive examination and prognosis has been the clear reaffirmation of how key quality-of-life factors are interrelated.

Case in point: the process of getting state university trustees to approve a campus on land near the Concord-Clayton border. After more than 10 years,

the battle was coming to a successful (for Contra Costa) conclusion, only to be temporarily stalled by a demand for assurances that the planned university would not substantially increase rush-hour traffic on already heavily traveled Ygnacio Valley Road.

As hard as they tried to ease traffic backups with changes like one-way streets and commute-hour regulations on turns off main thoroughfares, public works directors in county cities simply could not keep up with the ever-increasing number of vehicles using their roads.

This was not a situation confined to Contra Costa. The sharp increase in vehicle registrations occurred throughout most of California during the 1980s. "The annual addition of vehicles on state roads is incredible. There's no other word for it," said Neustadter.

According to Associated Press (AP) estimates, California's population is expected to increase 25 percent to 32.9 million by the year 2000 from the 26.4 million people residing in the state in 1987.

What that means for going places in the Golden State is ominous. AP figures that the number of licensed drivers in California will jump by 18 percent over the same period, increasing from 17.5 million to 20.6 million.

As of 1987 the state had 19 million vehicles which logged 196 billion miles annually—sufficient to

*The crush of traffic and the increase of vehicles is not unique to Contra Costa alone. The entire state of California is dealing with this dilemma as the population continues to multiply, adding more cars to the freeway systems. Solutions to the freeway problem will be found with the aid of mass transit. Photo by C. Curtis Corlew II*

make about 1,053 round trips to the sun or 410,287 round trips to the moon.

Transportation planners could not dwell for very long, however, on the idea of journeying to outer space. The slow pace of cars, trucks, and buses on county freeways quickly brought them down to earth.

At peak commute hours in the late 1980s, the average speed on urban freeways in California was 23 miles per hour, according to the AP report. That depressing fact was brought home to Contra Costa motorists who had to cope with slow traffic on heavily traveled arteries like Highways 80, 4, 680, and 24.

The urgency of finding significant traffic remedies was demonstrated by AP's forecast that the state's average freeway speed in the year 2000 would decline to 15 miles per hour during rush hours. Forcing that snail's pace, the AP explained, will be 30.3 million state-registered vehicles traveling 289.9 billion miles a year.

In order to dilute the negative impact of all the added vehicles taking to county roads, private- and public-sector officials have done their best to encourage the increased use of mass transit. Large office complexes such as Bishop Ranch in San Ramon and Airport Plaza in Concord initiated their own employee bus service to BART terminals.

But habits are hard to break. Getting residents out of their cars and into buses, BART trains, and

*Mass transit is a necessity in order to ease the burden on the freeway system. Though vehicle registration continues to increase, a variety of alternative transportation is available for most residents. Photo by Mark Gibson*

vans was a gradual process. An agency that has labored long with the private and public sectors to lighten the load on county roadways, RIDES for Bay Area commuters marked its 10th anniversary in 1987 and proudly proclaimed that it had:

—Provided assistance to more then 277,000 commuters.
—Placed 61,000 commuters into carpools.
—Organized more than 1,100 van pools.
—Saved $139 million on vehicle costs.
—Conserved 38 million gallons of fuel.
—Removed 40 million pounds of pollution from the air.
—Helped more than 1,500 employers provide ride-share services to their workers.

The effort to substantially reduce the huge number of single-occupant vehicles—especially during commute hours—was undertaken in a variety of ways.

Free carpool lanes at the westbound entrance to the Bay Bridge were a success, albeit a relative one given the crush of vehicles crossing that span seven days a week. High Occupancy Vehicle lanes were experimented with by Caltrans, the state transportation department, on heavily trafficked thoroughfares. Such lanes, it was hoped, would serve as an added incentive for the public to use mass transit.

It was an uphill marketing struggle for mass transit providers given the convenience and habit associated with that fixture of suburban living—the private automobile. The alternative to not waging the struggle was a grim one, however, given the gridlock that was fast approaching on city streets and freeways in Contra Costa.

Forced to raise fares to meet mounting overhead, BART was caught up in the dilemma of trying to regain riders ired by the higher cost of such travel. West county resident Nello Bianco, a veteran member of the system's board of directors, helped lead the campaign to add parking at overcrowded station sites and create improved bus connections to those points.

And to help soften the blow to Bay Area residents caused by increased fares, Bianco and his BART Board compatriots enacted special discount arrangements, including "children ride free" promotions at different times of the year.

The link between buses and BART was an important one in the ongoing campaign to unclog Contra Costa thoroughfares, particularly in areas like east county which were without actual rail service. Strategically located parking lots were constructed in these outlying regions, affording commuters and others the opportunity to hop on buses bound for BART terminals.

To remedy the complaints of frazzled commuters that bus service was far too time-consuming, carriers like the County Connection and AC Transit looked seriously into adding more express buses and eliminating stops that were proven to attract few if any riders.

Bus companies, a relatively new component of the county transportation picture, also sought to accommodate the needs of the growing private sector and the workers who comprise it. The County Connection, for example, was "changing from a bus company to a transportation company," according to its marketing director, Joyce Olson. Custom commuter services, organized and financed with the cooperation of business, were fast becoming a large segment of its enterprise.

*Above: Helicopter service at Buchanan Field in Concord provides efficient local flights throughout the county. Photo by Bob Rowan/Progressive Image*

*Left: Besides providing efficient and convenient express buses, County Connection also endorses other services for commuters, including van pools and employer-funded shuttles. Photo by Mark Gibson*

County Connection Director Carolyn Bovat, a former Clayton mayor, noted—on the occasion of the company's fifth anniversary in the summer of 1987—that "we have done what we were organized to do and we are operating well. We have a fleet of clean, well-maintained buses and a new facility [in Concord]. But times are changing."

Among the custom services endorsed by the board of the County Connection and mirrored by other area bus companies were van pools, express buses, and employer-funded shuttles. And to more swiftly move bus riders throughout the county, attention was focused on consolidating the many different regional systems—WestCAT (west Contra Costa), Tri-Delta Transit (east Contra Costa), AC Transit, and the County Connection.

In the case of busy downtown districts like those found in Walnut Creek, Concord, and Martinez, parking—or more accurately the lack of it—contributed to traffic tie-ups.

*Buchanan Field will be playing a pivotal role in Contra Costa as service in and out of the airport continues to increase, creating an accessible gateway for businesses and residents alike. Photo by Bob Rowan/ Progressive Image*

*Commuting by Amtrak is one of the various modes of transportation available to the county's residents. Photo by Roc DeWilde*

Planners and public works directors in those communities and others took multifaceted approaches to the problem: they created new lots and urged businesses, particularly retailers, to do the same. Tightened enforcement of parking laws was also part of the scenario.

The steps taken in Concord to ease the parking shortage in and around Salvio Pacheco Square were both ambitious and effective. A mid-rise parking structure was a striking component of the city's downtown redevelopment project in the early 1980s. Bank of America did its part to alleviate the parking shortage in the same area by including a huge parking garage in plans for its massive data processing and office center near the BART terminal.

Buchanan Field's importance to the overall transportation picture in the county cannot be emphasized enough. The start-up in 1986 of Pacific Southwest Airlines service between the Concord airport and Los Angeles will prove the catalyst for added scheduled service to other Western cities.

Careful not to overburden the already-busy airport or upset noise-conscious residents living near Buchanan, county officials exercised laudable care in approving new commercial flights in and out of the field. They did not have to be convinced, however, of the benefits of such services for county businesses and residents. The strong acceptance of the PSA flights and the mounting difficulties encountered in getting to the San Francisco and Oakland airports were proof enough.

Exotic solutions for solving the county's transportation woes, like double-decking Ygnacio Valley Road or running hydrofoils from west Pittsburg to the Port of San Francisco, were entertaining but far from practical. The idea of a Gateway route from the Caldecott Tunnel toward Alamo-Danville had become far too costly to rate as a reasonable concept; ditto, in the near future at least, opening another bore in the aging Caldecott. A light-rail system, utilizing the former Southern Pacific right-of-way between the south and central counties, is still very much a dream as Contra Costa nears the 1990s.

Mass transit, including Greyhound, Amtrak, BART, and the long list of local carriers, will be increasingly depended upon to move large numbers of people in, out, and through the county.

There are several reasons for optimism that this region is smoothing the way for the thousands of people using its roadways now and in the future.

In the west county, Highway 80 is due for widening from the Bay Bridge to Highway 4 near Pinole.

Well-traveled Highway 24, pictured here near Lafayette, will benefit from one of the many road improvement projects scheduled for the near future. This improvement is the expansion of the 680-24 freeway interchange, which will ease the crush of vehicles and will create a smoother transition for commuters. Photo by Mark Gibson

Start of construction on the North Richmond Bypass and completion of the John Knox Freeway are also very positive developments for Richmond-area travelers.

The addition of a lane in each direction on the Benicia Bridge will ease the Contra Costa-Solano commute until construction of a new span around the turn of the century.

Motorists from the Antioch-Pittsburg area are encouraged by progress toward lowering the Willow Pass grade near Concord and adding lanes to Highway 4.

Then, of course, there is the big one. Expansion of the 680-24 freeway interchange—expected to be completed in the early 1990s—will be the biggest vitamin yet for the movement of vehicles through the county.

The battles to get these projects started were long and expensive—very expensive. Heroes and heroines from all corners of society emerged from the complex approval process.

Traversing the county won't ever be as traffic-free as the horse-and-buggy days of the early 1900s. But with the remedies now on the horizon, Contra Costa residents can be justifiably hopeful of more tolerable motoring.

These aforementioned transportation improvements, unfolding and soon to unfold, signal an enhancement of the quality of life in the county—an enhancement of momentous proportions.

# CHAPTER 6

Quality of life in Contra Costa is enhanced by the many handsome homes in the various communities. This young family enjoys a quiet barbecue in their spacious backyard in Moraga. Photo by Bob Rowan/Progressive Image

# HOUSING

**T**rue: Contra Costa's progress story was built largely on the county's competitive advantages relative to housing.

Also true: Without solutions to the housing challenges now facing it, Contra Costa could be confronted with a dilution of quality of life and a drop-off of economic expansion. Fortunately, action on a number of fronts promises to ease concerns about housing availability and affordability countywide.

An abundance of what could generally be considered affordable housing was the chief catalyst in the 1970s and 1980s for business growth that enveloped the county. Major corporations looked to Contra Costa as a premier setting for large-scale office operations, aware that many of their employees already resided in the county and that those who didn't could find homes at relatively reasonable prices.

When compared to counties on the other side of San Francisco Bay, Contra Costa—until the late 1980s—offered home prices that were bona fide bargains. Although they still cost less than identical residences elsewhere in the region, these dwellings have grown significantly more expensive because of a combination of demographic and economic factors.

The well-documented business boom, increased household formations, and insufficient new construction all helped overburden the residential sector and forced prices upward. With demand running ahead of supply, pressure has predictably mounted on business and governmental

leaders to reverse the situation. When it comes to meeting housing challenges, speed is crucial, according to well-respected economists.

In its 1987 East Bay Economic and Demographic Forecast, Pacific Gas & Electric noted that, for the rest of this century, "the cities of central Contra Costa County will become financial and service centers. As these cities change from bedroom communities to employment centers, the demand for housing will remain strong. All this will occur in an economic environment of favorable interest rates and high per capita income, factors that will keep housing demand strong despite home prices that are well above state averages."

The pace at which home purchase and rental costs rose in Contra Costa during the last two decades was nothing short of astounding. Census data revealed that the median housing value in Contra Costa increased by 277 percent during the 1970s, from $25,000 to $94,300 per unit.

Figures from the 1985 county Housing Element portrayed the skyrocketing growth in the price of resale homes from 1976 to 1981. In the east county, the jump was 125 percent (from $35,389 to $79,610); in the west county, 126 percent (from $39,100 to $88,561); and in the central county, the focal point of Contra Costa business expansion, a whopping 137 percent (from $65,482 to $155,353).

Prices continued to rise, though at a somewhat slower rate, in the first half of the 1980s. In Walnut Creek and Concord, which have the largest housing turn-

over in the central county, 1985 sales prices of single-family detached homes averaged $121,000 and $92,000, respectively. Homes in the west county increased to an average of $110,500 that same year, according to figures furnished by the Contra Costa Council. In the rapidly growing east county, the average sales price in the middle of the decade neared the $90,000 mark, and was rising.

Even a quick check of the classified sections of East Bay newspapers revealed that condominium buyers and renters were confronted with similar inflationary prices.

*Above: Neighborhoods have evolved out of Contra Costa's housing developments, such as this area of Alamo, creating safe, well-kept communities for the area's residents. Photo by Mark Gibson*

Condos, billed by developers and sales agents as the affordable solution for first-time home buyers, also shot up in price. The reasons were similar to what was happening with the single-family home market: demand exceeding available supply and mounting overhead relative to construction.

In the areas with the most brisk commercial development—the central and south county—the cost of new condominiums flirted with or exceeded the $100,000 level during the late 1980s.

Contra Costa's working population is divided into two groups: those who both live and earn their wages here, and those who commute to jobs outside the county, principally in San Francisco. In terms of their housing requirements, persons in each category differ greatly because of geographic inclinations, income, levels of tolerance for commuting, and working addresses.

For the county's young and old—those feeling the severest pinch from escalation of housing prices—the choice of where to live is usually limited by minimal financial resources. Late-twentieth century phenomena such as a record divorce rate and the inclination of many people to delay marriage until their 30s and 40s contributed to increased demand for housing in Contra Costa. These added household formations were a key reason for a housing shortfall of 5,300 units faced by the county in early 1987. According to the Focus on Housing report of the Contra Costa Council, published that same year, overall residential vacancy rates for the region were less than 2 percent— well below the 4 to 5 percent recommended for a

healthy, efficiently operating housing market.

The tremendous diversity of county residents' backgrounds, financial resources, and life-styles is mirrored by the variety of housing that has taken shape here. This wide range of dwellings is both a prime asset of Contra Costa and a vivid testimony to the fine projects undertaken by residential builders in this area.

Six- and seven-figure estates in Blackhawk (Danville) and other upper-crust communities like Round Hill (Alamo) and nearby Diablo reflect the pinnacle of wealth in one of California's richest counties.

Single-family homes in the east, west, and central county, which sold new for less than $20,000 in the 1960s and early 1970s, are proof that affordable housing can be both attractive and enduring.

*In response to the increasing demand for rental housing, structures such as the Plaza Tower complex in Concord, pictured here, were built in an effort to supply much-needed apartments for county residents. Photo by Roc DeWilde*

As the 1990s came into view, the effort to make home ownership possible for middle-class Contra Costans continued at a high pitch. Nice, reasonably priced homes sprung from the soil by the thousands in the far eastern portions of the county in burgs like Oakley and Brentwood. The city of Antioch was projected by several astute economists to eventually become the second (after Concord) most populous city in the county.

In Martinez and, to the west, cities like Hercules, Pinole, and Richmond, neat, relatively affordable single-family homes were being produced in large volume.

In Concord mobile-home parks remained popular for people of all ages. Their attractiveness, both in terms of cost and minimal outdoor maintenance, was difficult to rival.

Evolution of the county economy, with primary emphasis in the 1970s and 1980s on white-collar job creation, had positive repercussions for the county housing market. For varying reasons, many of the new clerical workers and young professionals taking jobs in central and south Contra Costa spurned ownership of traditional single-family homes.

With these workers' number growing by staggering proportions, residential developers couldn't help but take notice and respond accordingly. New apartment construction, pretty much dormant in the central county during the early and mid-1980s, began to accelerate late in the decade.

The Bay Area Council, a San Francisco-based, non-profit organization representing the interests of business, acknowledged the trend as a product of such

Above: The west county town of Pinole still has ample room for future growth and development. Photo by Mark Gibson

Right: Neighborhoods evolved out of housing developments, creating a strong sense of community and family life. These youngsters take an afternoon stroll along a Concord street. Photo by Bob Rowan/ Progressive Image

Below: The Treat Commons apartments in Walnut Creek are conveniently located near the Pleasant Hill BART station. Photo by Roc DeWilde

factors as lower interest rates, availability of tax-exempt bond financing, tax incentives, high demand, and local acceptance of rental production. In the same report, the council warned that a change in even one of those circumstances could reverse the trend.

The proliferation of condominium and townhouse complexes in every portion of the county was expected but not, perhaps, to the degree it occurred. The push toward greater densities in residential construction and the presence of thousands of new upper-middle-class workers fueled the condo building boom.

Handsome, centrally located developments like Ellinwood in Pleasant Hill lured large numbers of single and married professionals. Condo complexes such as The Keys in Walnut Creek successfully marketed the recreational and social benefits of such a life-style.

The increased diversification of residential offerings has not changed the fact that the single-family, detached home remains the centerpiece of housing in the county. It—more than any other kind of dwelling—contributed to Contra Costa's population boom that started in the mid-1960s.

Homes of all shapes, sizes, and price ranges help give the county the diversified personality which makes it so desirable. Neighborhoods were born from the blueprints of developers who facilitated a housing rush in the central county during the late 1950s. In Concord, for example, Sun Terrace, Holbrook, and Dana Estates became distinctively separate addresses—each with nearby schools and shopping centers.

Although tract-type construction gave neighborhoods a certain sameness in outward appearance, it also assured equal levels of workmanship that home buyers came to appreciate. In the 1960s and early 1970s, ownership came cheap—compared to today's inflationary prices—and allowed individuals and families the chance to enhance and/or expand their dwellings. Through such projects, homes within the same development took on their own special identities.

Stipulations by local government on the design features of residential developments have become more plentiful and stringent over the last decade and a half. Intended to ensure a proper blend with existing single-family housing stock, they have succeeded—for the most part—in accomplishing that aim.

The splendid varieties of homes that adorn the county are products of many of the state's most distinguished developers. A number of them had extra incentive for creating the utmost in construction excellence in Contra Costa, for they, too, call this area home.

Long-established giants of the residential construction industry in Contra Costa are Ken Hofmann and Albert D. Seeno, Sr. The two veteran builders have left their imprint on thousands of dwellings in Northern California, a major portion of them located in this county.

*San Pablo Reservoir, located in the southwest section of Contra Costa, boasts crystal blue waters and breathtaking landscapes. Photo by Mark Gibson*

Thirty years old in 1987, the Hofmann Company has constructed more than 16,000 homes and apartments and developed commercial properties valued in excess of $50 million. The firm's headquarters is situated not far from Concord Avenue near the downtown of the county's largest city. Across from these corporate offices is the Big C Athletic Club, a Hofmann property frequented by successful businessmen from all over Contra Costa.

During the 1970s Hofmann's creative genius resulted in the emergence of Discovery Bay. The sprawling leisure community attracted working people as well as retirees to the easternmost reaches of the county. Complete with boating facilities and a championship golf course, the development achieved great success by capitalizing on the area's open

space and proximity to a water wonderland—the California Delta.

The Seeno name has been synonymous with the city of Pittsburg for more than a half-century. Unable to prosper in the fishing business, Seeno's father established a small construction firm in that east county city during the 1930s.

With the presence of Camp Stoneman, a bustling army base, Pittsburg's economy thrived during World War II. After that conflict ended, however, the city's business climate soured. It was during this period that Seeno played opportunist, purchasing huge amounts of acreage at prices impossible to turn down. The Seeno Company has since built more than 20,000 homes, more than half of them in the Pittsburg area. In the 1980s the firm got into commercial construction in a big, well-publicized way. Its "flagship project" was a large office complex located on Willow Pass Road in Concord. In the late 1980s officials announced plans to move their headquarters to Concord.

En route to becoming a model for residential development in California and the rest of the nation, Contra Costa has benefited from the professionalism of numerous builders. Peter Bedford, best known for the futuristic office buildings and shopping centers constructed by his Lafayette-based company, has also distinguished himself as a residential developer. Ken Behring, before undertaking Blackhawk and Canyon Lakes in the southern portion of this county, gained an outstanding reputation for designing country club communities in Florida. The Walnut Creek-based Smith Companies are responsible for several upscale housing developments in the wealthy communities of Lamorinda and along the 680 corridor in the south county.

Carlo Zocchi, operating out of Concord, and Earl Smith, who built many of the early homes in west Pittsburg, provided many county residents with first residences that did not overburden their family budgets. The same could be said for the efforts of east county developer Ralph Garrow.

These and other men who figured largely in the population explosion of Contra Costa combined to bring great diversity to the regional housing supply.

As Contra Costa became increasingly popular for people of all kinds of economic backgrounds, new housing construction grew much more expensive. Two main factors contributed to that rise: financing charges and land costs (including development fees).

Despite the declines enjoyed during the late 1980s, interest rates generally were on an upward spiral during the years that home building in the county occurred at a racehorse pace. The cost of money played havoc with both developers and home buyers. Builders, faced with longer processing times for subdivisions, passed along increased land prices to the consumer in the form of higher prices.

Would-be home buyers looked to government and the financial industry for fresh ideas on how they could afford to become homeowners.

In its "Growth Trends 1985," the Contra Costa Community Development Department explained the urgency of finding solutions to the cost spiral confronting home seekers.

The report noted that "an 'affordability gap' between the average price of a home and the median family income needed to qualify for a loan exists in Contra Costa County as elsewhere in the region and state. The costs of housing varies widely, with homes priced below $100,000 in the east county as well as average home prices in the $200,000 to $300,000 range in the central county. The price of an average home countywide is $154,000, which requires a

monthly income of about $4,200 to qualify for a loan, compared to a median family income in the region of $2,825."

"Focus on Housing," the research paper of the Contra Costa Council published in 1987, identified several possible solutions to the dilemma. Virtually all of them demand a cooperative effort by local government, state and federal governments, and the private sector.

Among those possible solutions were:

—Encouraging continuation and utilization of programs to assist lower-income and first-time home buyers (i.e., mortgage revenue bonds and tax-exempt financing, density bonuses, selective fee waivers).

—Responding to changed market demand and affordability problems by providing alternatives of smaller units and higher densities.

—Providing a funding base as broad as possible for needed public facilities benefiting the entire community (i.e., schools, roads, water, sewers, parks, fire facilities) rather than taxing only new home buyers.

—Creating and utilizing innovative funding mechanisms to provide funding for public facilities which do not impact solely the new home buyers.

—Maximizing the economy and efficiency of local services (i.e., consolidation of school districts).

The financial industry in California has been alert to the affordability problem confronting people of all ages. With the onset of lower interest rates during the latter part of the 1980s came a wide array of mortgage packages aimed at making home ownership affordable. Refinancing, a popular means for existing owners to lower their payments and period of payment, gained favor; variable rate packages, with the prevailing interest charges directly tied to the prime rate, became a vehicle increasingly used by first-time buyers.

In addition to the many different modes of creative home financing introduced into the marketplace

*Some families take it upon themselves to build their own homes, like these enterprising people in Oakley, thereby avoiding the additional cost of labor for the construction of new housing. Photo by Meri Simon*

by the private sector, government attempted to do its part with mortgage bond plans and tax-exempt financing. Examples of these efforts can be found primarily in the east and west county.

As available open space for new construction dwindled—especially in the central and southern portions of the county—increased housing densities were permitted, even encouraged, to meet the growing demand. Development of vacant land and redevelopment grew more in vogue as local governments pushed for increased housing stock near large employment centers in the county. Zoning laws were adjusted and building height ordinances reexamined in order to accomplish this goal. With prices of traditional single-family homes soaring and rental units becoming ever more costly, the public sector acceded to rethinking its stance regarding add-on units such as "mother-in-law cottages."

All of the aforementioned measures helped in relieving the jobs/housing imbalance in the county. Yet the growing snarls on streets and freeways were testimony that the challenge was an unending one. The major employment creation taking place in Concord-Walnut Creek and San Ramon-Pleasanton was creating new bedroom communities and commute patterns. A growing number of people from other counties were finding employment in Contra Costa. Both trends can be expected to continue into the 1990s as areas away from main employment centers offer the most reasonable housing prices.

Within the boundaries of Contra Costa, the east county figures to experience the strongest pace of new housing construction well into the twenty-first century. According to the 1980 Census, 41 percent of that region's housing stock was built after 1970—a figure certain to rise in the next few decades with the build-out of communities like Brentwood, Oakley, and Antioch.

*Even though much of the available space for residential construction has declined in recent years, the population of Contra Costa continues to grow, so the need for single-family dwellings will continue to increase. Photo by Roc De-Wilde*

The San Ramon-Alamo corridor will also blossom further as developers intensify their efforts in and around the foothills of Mount Diablo. Martinez can be counted on to sustain a significant level of residential construction activity. The same can be said for the greater Richmond area.

Nonetheless, a substantial portion of the new job holders in this county will venture elsewhere—to places like Tracy and Fremont and Vallejo and Fairfield—in search of affordable housing. The heightened commuter traffic into and out of Contra Costa will bring louder calls for crucial transportation remedies.

"Affordable housing can be a misleading term," said builder Carlo Zocchi. "You save money, sure, by moving to the outskirts of the county to buy a home. But how much is spent in gasoline and wear and tear on the family vehicle by driving an hour or more to and from work? All of this has to be taken into consideration."

The inflationary rise in the price of Contra Costa housing over the last few decades has created a trend of staying in one's residence longer and upgrading it as much as possible. Movement of people to other dwellings within the county has become increasingly rare.

This is a trend which applies to individuals and families on all levels of the income scale. "The wealthy, too, are very much interested in the affordability question," said Randy Smith, whose company focuses its development activity on high-income communities. "They realize they will be in their homes for a long time."

Those in the business of building homes in Contra Costa and those involved in other ways in the process generally are encouraged by moves being taken to make housing both more affordable and available.

The combination of the private and public sectors working together to solve these challenges appears the best prospect for progress in this all-important element of the Contra Costa life-style.

# CHAPTER 7

Students at Contra Costa College in San Pablo stroll through the school's campus as they make their way to and from classes. Contra Costa College is one of three colleges in the Contra Costa Community College District, which was first established in 1948. Photo by Bob Rowan/ Progressive Image

# EDUCATION

ducation is a word that has taken on a multitude of meanings in rapidly growing Contra Costa. The dramatic increase in the county's population during the last 25 years has combined with major expansion of the private sector to place many new and varied demands on our educational system—demands which are being answered in a number of ways.

Administrators and school board members have had to grapple with issues as complex as declining or rapidly rising enrollments; crucial additions or subtractions of course offerings; and teacher compensation in all of its various forms.

Alternatives to the traditional learning process have emerged inside and outside public education, springing from suggestions of parents, students, and interested persons in the general public. The result has been almost something for everyone in terms of classroom offerings.

The makeup of education in Contra Costa mirrors the splendid diversity of the county itself. The area is dotted by no less than 18 separate public school districts. Seven are unified, encompassing both elementary and secondary education. These are Antioch, Mt. Diablo, John Swett, Martinez, Pittsburg, Richmond, and San Ramon Valley.

Four are union elementary districts: Brentwood, Oakley, Byron, and Orinda. Each incorporated two or more districts in carving the present boundaries.

Two are union high school districts: Acalanes, serving the cities of

Lafayette, Moraga, Orinda, and Walnut Creek; and Liberty, situated in the far eastern portion of the county.

Five are elementary districts: Canyon, Knightsen, Lafayette, Moraga, and Walnut Creek.

Each district is governed by elected board members who conduct the business of their schools in accordance with state law. These people of wide-ranging backgrounds set policies and establish regulations; adopt annual budgets and approve expenditures; employ personnel of all levels; approve curriculum, textbooks, and courses of study; and make decisions on school sites, building plans, and contracts. A superintendent is hired by each board to administer the operation of the district.

The size of school districts vary significantly throughout the state as well as the county. In Contra Costa the smallest district is Canyon, near the town of Moraga. It had one school and 35 students as of 1987.

Easily the largest elementary and secondary school district in the county is Mt. Diablo Unified, based in Concord. With more than 31,000 students and 48 schools including seven high schools, it is the 10th-largest district in California. Encompassing most of the central county, MDUSD is a blending of the old and new in terms of physical properties and instructional philosophies. The demographic composition of this administration, faculty, staff, and student body has all the characteristics of an intriguing melting pot.

Because of the 1960s and 1970s population explosion in cities like Concord, Pleasant Hill, and Walnut Creek, Mt. Diablo was forced to grow perhaps faster than it wanted. Drop-offs in student enrollment, beginning in the late 1970s, prompted MDUSD trustees to implement a painful plan of school closures. Among the victims was Pleasant Hill High, one of the central county's oldest high schools.

Indicative of the changing mission of Contra Costa's largest district, one of the closed schools—Crawford Village Elementary in Concord—was converted into Loma Vista Adult Education Center, and the facility thrives today. Two other MDUSD elementary schools have been refocused in the direction of a "Back to Basics" approach to learning.

The Contra Costa County Office of Education, headquartered in Pleasant Hill, was first established in 1852 by mandate of the state legislature. In the early days, the county superintendent directly supervised all of the schools in his jurisdiction. To do so, he frequently made long rides by horseback to communities throughout the area. The county superintendent then was responsible for the curriculum of the schools and the certification of teachers. Over many years, the office changed into essentially a fiscal and clerical arm of the state.

Today the county Office of Education acts as a unifying umbrella for the 18 districts. Among the tasks

of the county superintendent are the checking of school district budgets and accounts; calculating income of the districts; reporting enrollment figures; and operating numerous educational programs for children and adults. These include special education, occupational preparation, and schooling for wards of the juvenile court and adults in jail.

The freedom to manage their own schools—given by the state to the individual districts—has been a key factor in making county schools effective for their particular situations. Curricula as well as extracurricular activities vary according to the community. Steadily climbing test scores of elementary as well as secondary students in the overwhelming majority of Contra Costa schools are testimony to the fact that local management of education is a correct course.

Nearly 117,000 young people in kindergarten through 12th grade attended county public schools in 1987. As of that year, approximately 24,000 people were employed by public education agencies in Contra Costa. The total payroll for the public schools in the region was $348 million.

Well over $20 billion in state, federal, and local funds were spent for elementary and secondary public education in California during the 1987-1988 school year. Most of that revenue—nearly 70 percent—came from state income and sales taxes. The federal government contributed around 5 percent, with most of that money earmarked for child nutrition, special education, and educationally disadvantaged children. The remainder of school district revenue came from local prop-

*Above: These young boys play a game of catch in the schoolyard of Canyon School. Photo by Roc DeWilde*

*Facing page, top: Adult education is a top priority in Contra Costa. From day and evening classes in undergraduate and graduate studies to a large variety of vocational training opportunities, many residents take advantage of the continuing education programs in the county. These students take a moment to compare notes at Los Medanos College in Pittsburg. Photo by Bob Rowan/Progressive Image*

*Facing page, center: Besides teaching children the necessary academic skills and lessons, the educational system provides each student the opportunity to learn about teamwork and friendship with their schoolmates. Students at Hillview Elementary in Pittsburg participate in a tug-of-war contest at the annual school Olympics. Photo by C. Curtis Corlew II*

erty taxes and other sources including the state lottery.

Despite improvement in funding, California is still significantly behind the national average in expenditures per pupil. Around 35 percent of combined state and local resources goes to public education in California. Nonetheless, Contra Costa school districts have succeeded in providing the young people they serve with the tools to become productive members of society. They have accomplished this by careful allotment of funding and manpower, and by being amenable to change.

Private and parochial schools have figured prominently in the diversification of educational opportunities in the county. These institutions, providing both elementary and secondary education, have proven attractive to parents seeking to provide their children with added dimensions to the learning process. Smaller classes, more specialized curricula, extra attention to discipline, and, in the case of church schools, religious instruction, are all incentives for taking this direction.

Athenian, Doris Eaton, and Palmer are examples of well-established private elementary schools in the county. Together with the numerous church-sponsored elementary schools, including the large network of Catholic schools, they represent a respected alternative to the public school system.

Primarily reliant on tuition fees to fund their operations, private schools have been the beneficiaries of the county business boom which has brought thousands of new executives and their families to Contra Costa.

"Location is a critical factor. There's no doubt about that," said Adrian Mendes, long-time administrator of the Palmer School. "The two-salary household has also contributed significantly to the success of this kind of education. We see it every day—parents dropping their children at school on the way to jobs in San Francisco and Oakland.

"In terms of classroom offerings, we give our students courses which challenge them to the fullest. Individual attention and small classes help these students meet that challenge. There is definite structure to the ex-

*Right: The Happy Days Learning Center in Lafayette, owned and directed by May Yen, provides a fun and caring environment for pre-school age children. Photo by Roc De-Wilde*

*Left: The Christian Center School in Pittsburg is one of many private elementary schools in Contra Costa. These young students gather for the first day of classes. Photo by Meri Simon*

perience here—a structure that parents realize is beneficial to learning."

On the high school level, private and parochial institutions have, for the most part, more than just met a static need. As the 1980s came to a close, a number of them were either expanding their facilities or planning to do so in the near future.

De La Salle High School in Concord, for example, is adding an entire new academic wing which will enable it to accommodate 200 more students.

Throughout the county, several secondary schools with a nondenominational Christian orientation emerged during the 1970s and 1980s and experienced steadily increasing enrollments.

These schools, it should be underscored, pride themselves on providing special kinds of education which emphasize academic skills as well as moral and spiritual enrichment.

The private secondary schools of Contra Costa choose not to detach themselves from the rest of society. In academic as well as athletic competition, they have enthusiastically engaged in competition against squads representing public schools. Some county-based private and parochial high schools have sponsored summer sessions attended by students from a wide spectrum of educational backgrounds.

The approach to private-school financing is understandably challenging. Because of their relative newness, such institutions in this region have had to acquire the fine points of "fund raising on the job," so to speak. Nonetheless they have succeeded admirably by being alert to new sources of assistance. To their credit, the county's private and parochial schools have tried hard to limit tuition increases while offering help to financially disadvantaged students. On both counts, their efforts have met with mostly favorable results.

When it comes to the realm of higher education, Contra Costa residents have a wide range of outstanding institutions from which to choose. These colleges and universities run the gamut of possible affiliations including public, church-affiliated, and private schools. The reputation of the Bay Area as a citadel of learning has unquestionably extended to this county.

The Contra Costa Community College District, headquartered in Martinez, has grown dramatically since its formation in 1948. The district now encompasses three self-contained campuses: Contra Costa College in San Pablo; Diablo Valley College in Pleasant Hill; and Los Medanos College in Pittsburg. Together these institutions serve a diversified student population of more than 37,000.

From very humble beginnings represented by a few temporary buildings in Martinez and the Richmond Shipyards (the birthplace of Contra Costa College), the CCCCD is now among the 10-largest entities of its kind in California. The community colleges have blossomed along with the county, offering programs enabling students to extend their education or pursue meaningful private-sector career opportunities.

*Above: The 26th Annual Walnut Creek Swim Conference was held at Acalanes High School in Lafayette, utilizing the school's impressive facilities. Photo by Roc DeWilde*

During the mid-1980s the district joined with Cal State Hayward Extended Education and UC Berkeley Extension in a cooperative attempt to bring the benefits of higher education directly to the workplace.

Thus was born the Center for Higher Education in the bustling Bishop Ranch business development at San Ramon. Corporate tenants at Bishop Ranch, including Pacific Bell, Chevron, and Beckman Instruments, welcomed with open arms these colleges and universities into their midst. Conveniently scheduled classes permit businessmen and women to acquire the learning that they need to advance in their chosen fields.

At the center, Diablo Valley College offers a wide variety of courses based on the needs of the community. These include accounting, computerized accounting, computer programming, career planning, high-technology office skills, English, management and supervision, mathematics, psychology, and word processing.

Careful not to duplicate academic offerings at San Ramon with those of Diablo Valley College, Cal State and UC Berkeley provide instruction in a diversity of subjects geared toward both personal and professional development. Formats vary from evening and day classes to one-day programs.

The maturation of Contra Costa's business sector has been a catalyst for many colleges and universities to initiate adult education programs in the county. Golden Gate University, the University of Phoenix, National University, and the University of San Francisco are among the institutions that have acted on their inclination that this is a region ripe for a wide range of adult learning experiences. In virtually every case, classes are held in a business environment. Instructors/professors bring to the classroom a significant wealth of on-the-job experience.

Jack Carhart, a nearly lifelong county resident who became chancellor of the CCCCD in the late 1980s, is keenly aware of the different reasons county residents pursue higher education. As Los Medanos College's first president, he directed development of a curriculum that would be attentive to a wide spectrum of goals.

"Our [community] colleges were built to serve the entire county and its residents," said Carhart. "Each one has a highly acclaimed transfer program to all public and private four-year colleges and universities. More than 50 vocational programs are offered at our various campuses, many in public service areas like police, fire, nursing, and dental programs. We are con-

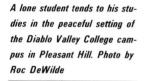

*A lone student tends to his studies in the peaceful setting of the Diablo Valley College campus in Pleasant Hill. Photo by Roc DeWilde*

tinually reexamining our curricula in order to respond to the needs of the growing private sector in Contra Costa."

The community college district is the oldest component of an ever-increasing network of public institutions of higher learning in the county.

Proving that old schools never die or completely fade away, officials at California State University at Hayward selected the former Pleasant Hill High facility as the site for its Contra Costa campus which first opened in 1981.

The Contra Costa campus of Cal State Hayward offers bachelor degrees in liberal studies, business administration, English, human development, and criminal justice administration. Master degree programs are available in counseling, business administration, public administration, and education. Credentials are awarded in elementary and secondary teaching, administrative services, and instruction of the learning handicapped.

Indicative of the increasing popularity of adult education throughout the county, enrollment at the Cal State Hayward campus more than quadrupled during the first four years of its existence. The average age of students there is 30. As is the case with the community colleges, the campus in Pleasant Hill—because of its public-funding base—has a modest schedule of student fees.

Saint Mary's College of California, founded in San Francisco in 1863 and relocated to the Moraga Valley in 1928, is the oldest of the institutions of higher learning based in Contra Costa. The college, administered and operated by the Christian Brothers teaching order of the Roman Catholic Church, has a storied past that includes a football dynasty in the 1930s and 1940s and service as a navy pre-flight school during World War II.

Since its transfer to control of the Christian Brothers in 1868, Saint Mary's has held steadfastly to

*Saint Mary's College, originally established in 1863 in San Francisco, moved to the Moraga Valley in the late 1920s. Approximately 2,000 students attend the college, receiving a sound liberal arts education, strengthened by Catholic ideals. Photo by Mark Gibson*

cally under the presidential administration of Brother Mel Anderson.

Extended education programs, including paralegal, management, and health-services administration, have given the college an important presence in cities throughout the Bay Area. A wide array of MBA curricula have attracted ever-increasing numbers of working adults to the Saint Mary's campus. An upswing in the need for teachers fostered higher enrollment for the School of Education during the 1980s. The School of Science is proud of its reputation of sending many graduates on to advance study and careers in professional fields.

Since its establishment in 1964 by Georgia L. Morrison and Lind M. Higgins, John F. Kennedy University has achieved a reputation for outstanding efforts in the area of adult education. For its first 22 years, JFKU confined its efforts to undergraduate upper-division and graduate learning.

In the latter half of the 1980s, the Orinda-based university of about 2,000 students introduced a lower-division liberal arts program heavily focused on a study of the classics. That momentous step, the administration believed, was in line with the university's stated mission of making lifelong learning available to serious students.

Within John F. Kennedy University are five schools: Liberal and Professional Arts; Graduate School of Professional Psychology; School of Management; School of Law; and the Graduate School for the Study of Human Consciousness. In addition to its Orinda campus, JFKU holds classes days and evenings at several other Bay Area locations and on nine military bases in California.

Reflective of the institution's innovative stance is its "Access to Learning" program. Students from more than 40 states and Canada are able to use their personal computers to complete an MBA degree or a certificate curriculum without leaving their homes. John F. Kennedy University seems destined to relocate to a more spacious setting in the future, very possibly outside the county. Its influence, however, is sure to be maintained here.

Changes are certain in the composition of Contra Costa education during the years ahead.

The most stirring development of the new decade could well be construction of a branch campus of the California State University at Concord. As the 1990s approached, momentum mounted for building this facility.

Although major questions still abound about the initial format of this institution, there is agreement and enthusiasm over the benefits to be reaped by the county and its residents from having a CSU campus.

For several local legislators and businesspeople, the strong possibility of construction of this campus is yet another unquestionable indicator that Contra Costa has indeed come of age.

three guiding principles: Catholic fundamentals, a liberal arts foundation, and Lasallian philosophy. (Saint John Baptist De la Salle, founder of the Christian Brothers, espoused an educational system which emphasized a strong rapport between students and teachers and encouraged enrollment by young people from all strata of society, especially the poor.)

Saint Mary's is one of a few colleges and universities in California with a Great Books core curriculum. All undergraduate students at the college, regardless of major, are required to be versed in the great literary works of mankind.

As of the late 1980s, the undergraduate student population at Saint Mary's stood at slightly more than 2,000. About half that number were boarders. Of the other thousand people, a significant portion were commuter students from Contra Costa County. For several consecutive years, nearby Diablo Valley College proved to be Saint Mary's largest single source of students.

With the introduction of coeducation (in 1970) and graduate and extended education curricula (both in 1975), enrollment at Saint Mary's has risen dramati-

# CHAPTER 8

From idyllic scenery and healthy outdoor recreation to landscaped office
parks and sprawling shopping centers,
Conta Costa County offers a complete
and full life-style for its ever-growing
population. Photo by C. Curtis Corlew II

# THE GOOD LIFE

I t's understandable that Contra Costa residents might feel that they just about have it all.

The meteoric growth of the county has brought with it a myriad of benefits— everything from sprawling regional shopping centers to handsome entertainment facilities to beautiful parks and restaurants.

Now one of the more affluent and populous regions of California, "CC" —as newspaper headlines often call it—has acquired a multidimensional, special personality all its own.

The great variance in income levels and life-styles of people who live and work in this county has provided a bonanza for retailers. Upper-crust department stores, discount houses, and thrift shops have all discovered here a dynamic marketplace for their goods.

Leisure activity comes in many different forms with wide-ranging fee schedules. Biking and hiking are free for the partaking. Private and public golf courses make for a game that can suit one to a tee. Swimming pools come in all shapes and sizes. Tennis courts are just about everywhere.

Movie houses have sprung up with ticket prices and feature films to suit virtually every budget and interest. Live entertainment is plentiful. Comedy clubs, indoor and outdoor theaters, and hotel lounges provide lots of options for spending a fun evening.

Limousine services thrive in this county. So do economy rental car agencies. Fancy eating establishments, many of them with San Francisco connections, have an appreciative, sophisticated clientele in Contra Costa. But burgers and fries also appeal to the people here, and fortunately just about every fast-food outlet imaginable is available to choose from.

In a fast-growing area like this one, selection is all-important—regardless of whether one is seeking retail goods, health care, or recreational vehicles.

The great mix of shopping centers in Contra Costa is testimony to the county's demographic diversity. Concord, the county's largest city, reflects the great mix of retailing in Contra Costa.

Sunvalley regional shopping center, developed on former marshland, was opened in 1967. Over the last two decades, it has matured into a mall that is now a model for developers and retailers nationwide. With four strong anchor tenants (Sears, J.C. Penney, Macy's, and Emporium-Capwell) and more than 100 smaller stores offering just about every kind of item known to mankind, Sunvalley draws customers from all over Northern California. During the last several years, Sunvalley has also evolved into a dining and entertainment hub. Restaurants of all kinds fill the upper and lower levels of the center. A movie theater and ice-skating rink are available for recreation seekers.

Minutes away by car from Sunvalley is the Willows Shopping Center. Perhaps more than any other mall in Contra Costa, the Willows has exhibited a multitude of personalities during its more than 10 years of existence.

Instituted as a specialty center comprised mostly of boutiques and rather exotic restaurants, the Willows grappled with an identity dilemma from the beginning.

Through changes of ownership and several turnovers of tenants, the focus of the Willows was redirected toward paying heightened attention to consumers living near the mall. Accordingly an increasing number of shops emerged with prices and goods within the reach of the middle class. Kept in this transition was the center's emphasis on making shopping enjoyable. The Willows' distinctive look and generous sprinkling of dining establishments contribute to a memorable experience. The music emanating from the studios of KKIS Radio adds to the ambience. So, too, does the presence of the city-operated theater which offers live entertainment year-round. Having found its market niche serving the middle class as well as those in more affluent income situations, the Willows appears to be in a position to grow along with the rest of Contra Costa.

*Facing page, top left: Boating along the pristine delta waterways is only one of the many outdoor activities to be enjoyed by county residents and visitors alike. Photo by Jordan Coonrad*

*Facing page, top right: Park and Shop, the oldest shopping center in Concord, boasts a wide variety of goods and services for the area's shoppers, as well as an assortment of restaurants. Photo by Roc DeWilde*

*Below: The setting sun casts long shadows across the greens of a golf course in Concord. Photo by Roc DeWilde*

*Below: KKIS Radio has been serving the county since its inception in 1948. Program Director Sean McMahon is one of the station's personalities, providing listeners with a variety of music and news. Photo by Roc DeWilde*

Not far from Sunvalley and the Willows, near the revived downtown sector of Concord, is Park and Shop, the city's oldest major shopping center. Constructed in the late 1950s, Park and Shop mirrors the retailing era in which it was founded. Comprised primarily of sprawling one-story structures, Park and Shop possesses the rather unique architectural feature of having stores and restaurants which face out in four directions. Among its long-standing inhabitants are the headquarters of Wentling Camera and Video and the Capri Theater. Though it no longer has a supermarket, Park and Shop had that kind of anchor tenant for a significant portion of its history. Other key "draws," in addition to Wentling's and the theater, have primarily been in the realm of soft goods. Prone to aging, like everything else, this granddaddy of Concord retailing received a needed facelift in the late 1980s that included reworking of the center's parking alignment and traffic flow.

Anchor tenants appearing on the Park and Shop scene relatively recently are Ross (a discount clothing outlet) and Levitz (a massive discount furniture chain). Among the mall's more notable occupants that have come and gone over time are Woolworth's, Grants, Liberty House, and C.W. Markus Hardware. In the last couple of years, the center has added a number of popular fast-food restaurants including McDonald's, Burger King, and an Emil Villa's Barbecue Pit. Through all the changes, Park and Shop's pull as a shopping center for the masses has been greatly en-

hanced, proof that this kind of center is anything but a dinosaur.

Concord's growth explosion of the 1960s and 1970s began from the downtown core area and moved in virtually every direction. Predictably, shopping centers—many of them anchored by supermarkets and drugstores—were developed to serve residents in particular parts of the community. Today these neighborhood malls, which range in size from Clayton Valley and the Vineyard to Dana Plaza and El Monte, typify the convenient, suburban life-style which so many people find attractive. In the older sections of Contra Costa's largest city, along Monument Boulevard and Port Chicago Highway, long-standing shopping centers represent the hub of day-to-day activity for their neighborhoods.

What has transpired in Concord relative to the brisk retail activity enveloping the community is typical of a pattern happening throughout the county. Soaring populations in the east, south, west, and central county were the catalyst for huge waves of shopping center development during the 1970s and 1980s. Retailers with regional and national reputations found Contra Costa to be an area with huge potential. Careful to thoroughly analyze prospective marketplaces before embarking on an expansionist course, these developers found the county, its cities, and its neighborhoods ideal sites for serving all kinds of consumers.

Naturally, factors like household income, housing prices, and proximity to major transportation arteries dictated, to a large degree, the complexion and composition of new retail development. In the case of numerous county communities, the presence of two distinctly different groups—residents and nonresident workers—had to be taken into account. The growing prev-

*Above: TR's Bar & Grill, located in Concord at the corner of Salvio Street and Concord Avenue, features an attractive outdoor setting for its customers. Photo by Bob Rowan/Progressive Image*

*Far left: Along with a wide selection of major retail centers to choose from, Contra Costa also offers smaller, more specialized stores. Here, shoppers browse through the boutiques at the Danville Hotel. Photo by Mark Gibson*

*Left: Complete with a movie theater and an ice skating rink, the Sunvalley Mall houses over 100 different stores, providing a countless number of goods and services for its customers. Photo by Roc DeWilde*

Broadway Plaza Shopping Center in Walnut Creek has undergone numerous notable changes since its emergence in 1951 with J.C. Penney and Sears as anchors. Both retailers have long since left Broadway because of the development of regional malls to the north (Sunvalley) and south (Stoneridge).

With Walnut Creek and such adjoining communities as Alamo and Lafayette acquiring reputations as affluent, sophisticated suburbs, Broadway has made a well-planned, successful effort over time to attract and keep an upscale clientele.

As the 1980s neared a close, Broadway Plaza heartily welcomed Nordstrom, the service-oriented, soft goods department store, to its lineup of fine retailers. With I. Magnin, Emporium-Capwell, county-based McCaulou's, and Mervyn's for Kids preceding it at the Walnut Creek downtown mall, Nordstrom brass realized that Broadway was indeed the proper place for entry into the choice Contra Costa market. With the aforementioned larger stores and a wide range of eating establishments and shops, Broadway has carved a viable, valuable market in the face of stiff competition on all its flanks.

In the last decade and a half, a great number of area shopping centers have been constructed in response to the public's demand for convenience and its needs for particular goods and services in a wide variety of price ranges.

Among the relative newcomers to the Contra Costa retail scene are County East (Antioch), Alamo Plaza, Crow Canyon Commons (San Ramon), the Livery and Mercantile (Danville), and rapidly expanding sub-regional centers in Hercules and Pinole. Each has its own special tenant mix. Each was born of a population boom expected to continue to one degree or another in the future.

The influx of new stores and shopping centers into the county has had a profound effect on the proliferation of service enterprises. Financial institutions, restaurants, professional offices, automobile service and repair stations, and health clubs have all benefited from proximity to growing population centers.

Contra Costa residents no longer have to make trips to San Francisco, Monterey, and the like to find first-class dining spots. In the 1970s the county began to be dotted by restaurants with a wide variety of cuisines. A large percentage of them settled in or near the busy business districts of fast-growing cities like Concord, Walnut Creek, and San Ramon in hopes of capturing a brisk lunchtime trade. Names like California Cafe, Pacific Fresh, Spiedini's, the Front Room, Posh, and Pacific Cafe quickly became linked with the suit-and-briefcase crowd in Contra Costa.

Ethnic eateries, offering such culinary delights as Chinese, Japanese, French, Mexican, and Greek food demonstrated that the region was rapidly becoming chic and cosmopolitan. The bar and grill, a trade-

*Broadway Plaza in Walnut Creek, with its tastefully decorated storefronts, attractive landscaping, and fine retailers, has created a refined, upscale atmosphere for its customers to enjoy. Photo by Mark Gibson*

alence of multiple-income households was also an important consideration.

The Michigan-based Taubman Company, owner and operator of Sunvalley in Concord, noted relatively early the formation of very separate marketplaces in Contra Costa. The results of its extensive demographic studies were two new regional shopping centers built to meet the need of residents in opposite ends of the county. Richmond's Hilltop Mall, which opened in 1975 along busy Interstate 80, attracts shoppers from its home city of Richmond as well as from nearby communities in Alameda and Solano counties. Stoneridge Mall, located at the crossroads of Freeways 580 and 680 in Pleasanton, made its debut around the beginning of the 1980s. Strategic location was an important magnet for the Taubman Company, which correctly surmised that the mall would be frequented by individuals from both the southern sections of Contra Costa and Alameda counties. Having two major employment centers—Bishop Ranch (San Ramon) and Hacienda Park (Pleasanton)—in close proximity to the center proved a key catalyst in Stoneridge's acceptance by generally well-to-do customers.

mark of the San Francisco life-style, appeared on the county scene with the likes of Crogan's (Walnut Creek), TR's (Concord), and LeBeau's (Martinez).

Contra Costans, desirous of atmosphere with their meals, have numerous options from which to make a selection. Those who like a waterfront setting might well lean toward places like the Riverview (Antioch) or the Albatross (Martinez). At Boundry Oak (Walnut Creek) or the Moraga Country Club, one can dig into a steak or club sandwich while watching golfers take their swings. For elegance, places like La Tourelle (Lafayette), the Savoy (Pleasant Hill), and Casa Orinda are there to fill the bill.

A taste of the Old West is available in Clayton, where both the Pioneer Inn and the Clayton Saloon vibrantly capture the cowboy spirit of yesterday. Nostalgia buffs can also delight in the mood of restaurants like Richmond's Hotel Mac; the Warehouse in quaint Port Costa; and Amato's in Martinez.

Elevation of Contra Costa's hotel industry to new levels of service and variety is undisputable. Cities like Antioch, Concord, Martinez, Pleasant Hill, San Ramon, and Walnut Creek all got into the tourist business in bigger and different ways during the 1980s.

Antioch, located at the mouth of California's scenic Delta waterways, drew the interest of hotel developers who located two large inns along Highway 4 near the County East Shopping Center.

For many decades, the Concord Inn was the lone major hotel in the county's most populous city. By the close of the last decade that sprawling community was the site of Hilton, Holiday Inn, and Sheraton hotels. Plans for a Red Lion convention center and hotel near Buchanan Field, though stalled temporarily in the late 1980s, were eventually expected to come to fruition. Also ballyhooed for the future were hotel-restaurants to be located within walking distance of BART stations in Concord and Pleasant Hill.

While hotel/motel construction in Martinez and Pleasant Hill was geared for the most part to accommodate individual travelers and smaller groups, a varying strategy was detectable in Walnut Creek where a large Ramada Renaissance Hotel was built near the 680-242 freeway interchange and the local BART terminal. Within Sunset Development's massive Bishop Ranch business park in San Ramon a large Marriott Hotel took shape.

Contra Costa's quality of health care, like its quality of schools, is a significant reason for the county's attractiveness as a place to live and work. The Oakland-based Kaiser Permanente system responded to the need of serving the masses by opening hospitals and clinics in Walnut Creek, Martinez, Antioch, and Richmond.

As with most everything else in their lives, county residents are fortunate to have a wide range of choices when it comes to hospitals and convalescent facilities.

*For a delightful dining experience with the ambience of the French countryside, the Tourelle Cafe & Restaurant in Lafayette is a must. Photo by Bob Rowan/Progressive Image*

Mt. Diablo Medical Center in Concord and John Muir Memorial Hospital in Walnut Creek have achieved national reputations for advances in health care. Both institutions, originally intended as community hospitals, have expanded dramatically during the last decade in response to the population boom encompassing the county. As could be figured, the two state-of-the-art facilities have become widely known with specific programs: John Muir, for its trauma center; and Mt. Diablo, for an innovative unit which treats the causes and effects of alcoholism.

In the fast-growing east county, Los Medanos Community Hospital in Pittsburg and Delta Memorial Hospital in Antioch significantly increased their physical plants to accommodate increased demand. Contra Costa County Hospital in Martinez and Brookside Hospital in San Pablo serve a wide geographic area inclusive of the west county and beyond.

Be it boating, bocce ball, bingo, tennis, or softball, county residents are blessed with lots of opportunities to fill their leisure hours. Municipal, East Bay, and state parks have given credence and depth to the meaning of the "Great Outdoors." Outstanding city-operated aquatic complexes like Cowell Park in Concord and Heather Farms in Walnut Creek permit young and old alike to get into the swim of things.

If it's not sports that suits one's fancy, Contra Costa's social fiber is resplendent with clubs and organizations of every description and purpose. Gardeners, gem collectors, metal-detector owners, model railroad buffs, and quilters can all find local groups of enthusiasts who share their interests.

Churches of all shapes, sizes, and denominations help give substance to life in Contra Costa. They are the source of numerous activities and exemplify goodwill to the less fortunate among us.

Groups like the Salvation Army, Red Cross, Contra Costa Volunteer Bureau, the Contra Costa Crisis and Suicide Prevention Service, and the county Assistance League provide hope and tangible benefits to those in need of them. The multitude of service clubs that operate within the county's boundaries have been responsible for upgrading the quality of life in Contra Costa.

The young and the old are able to take advantage of seemingly endless opportunities for camaraderie. Athletic competition and other recreation abound for both societal groups. Little leagues have become big leagues all over the area.

Advances in public transportation make leisure activities more accessible for the many people who wish to partake of them. In such diverse communities as Rossmoor in Walnut Creek, Pittsburg, and Martinez, senior citizens find fun and strength in numbers.

Perhaps the most striking barometer of how far the county's life-style has come can be found in the arena of the performing arts. The Concord Pavilion, which made its debut in 1975, has a glowing record

*Above: A barefoot waterskier delights in an afternoon of sun and fun along the county's waterways. Photo by Jordon Coonrad*

*Top, right: Clayton's Pioneer Inn is a favorite place for diners seeking the flavor of the Old West. Photo by Roc De-Wilde*

*Center, right: Mt. Diablo Medical Center in Concord is strategically located in the central part of the county and features extensive facilities throughout the hospital, such as this state-of-the-art equipment in the radiology department. Courtesy, Mt. Diablo Medical Center*

*Bottom, right: A parent and child pause for a rest beneath a majestic oak tree on Dinosaur Hill in Pleasant Hill as evening light falls over Contra Costa. Photo by Roc DeWilde*

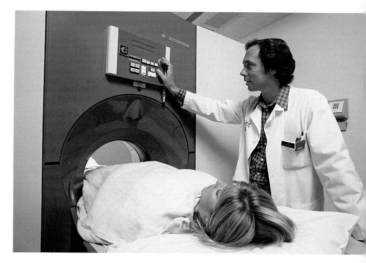

of bringing big-name entertainment to Contra Costa. Throughout the region, acting troupes bring joy to others.

As the curtain began to drop on the 1980s, it appeared that the county would soon be home to a regional performing arts center (in downtown Walnut Creek) and the Berkeley Shakespeare Theater (in Orinda).

Unquestionably, Contra Costa has become a happening place—one that seeks to offer something for everyone. Its outstanding quality of life is a tribute to the tireless efforts of countless individuals and organizations. To them, eternal gratitude is due.

# CHAPTER 9

*Dusk falls over the glittering skyline of San Francisco. Photo by Jordan Coonrad*

# THE BIGGER BAY AREA PICTURE

To many people outside of the region, the Bay Area is San Francisco.

Such a simplistic view is somewhat comprehensible and surely predictable given the widely held perception of the City as a world-class urban center with all the attributes that go with that lofty designation.

Yet it must be underscored again and again that the Bay Area has achieved greatness by being San Francisco and more—much more. Stretching some 100 miles north to south, and east to west from the edge of the San Joaquin Valley to the blue Pacific, the fabled region is the magnificent sum of many splendid parts.

There is little if any argument that San Francisco is the centerpiece of the Bay Area. With its enchanting topography, weather, and wide-ranging entertainment attractions, the City is a magnet for visitors from all over the world.

When it comes to charisma, San Francisco is a match for any city on the planet. The Golden Gate Bridge, the cable cars, and Chinatown are the kind of stuff that makes for best-selling postcards. Political and sports history has been repeatedly made in this city to which Tony Bennett paid permanent tribute in song. World leaders—the stature of kings, queens, popes, and presidents—regularly place San Francisco on their itineraries.

The location of San Francisco, central to the West Coast and at the gateway to the Pacific Ocean, provides a cosmopolitan flair that permeates the life of

the entire Bay Area. The population of the region reflects the stirring demographic trends expected to accelerate during the twenty-first century throughout the United States and especially in California.

The number of people of Hispanic and Asian backgrounds taking residence in Northern California has risen significantly in the last half of this century. Contra Costa and the other eight counties generally considered to comprise the Greater Bay Area have experienced the impact of this major development. Governmental agencies, educators, and employers have appropriately refocused their efforts to take into account these constituencies.

For virtually all of its history, San Francisco has been a melting pot of individuals of very different ethnic backgrounds and races. The list of individuals who have served as mayor of the City shows that to be true.

The blossoming of other parts of the Bay Area, helped to a large degree by pioneer projects like construction of the Golden Gate and Bay bridges, is a tribute to the true grit of countless individuals. The risktakers responsible for the California Gold Rush of the mid-1800s left a special legacy to future inhabitants of this splendid region. Their hard work and perseverance was mirrored in the marvelous maturation first of San Francisco, and then of the entire Bay Area.

A bit lost in the ongoing ballyhoo of San Francisco as a top tourist town are the other, very important components of the City's economy—the multitude of corporations that give employment and prosperity to thousands upon thousands of Bay Area residents.

Best symbolized perhaps by the towering Transamerica Pyramid which reaches into the often fog-shrouded heavens, San Francisco's private sector has been on the ascent since very early in this century. Headquarters for corporations as diverse as banks, oil refiners, and retailers are the cornerstone for this thriving business community.

The Port of San Francisco and related maritime enterprises have long been key elements in determining the City's state of economic health. The last couple of decades have catapulted these trade-oriented businesses into renewed prominence. Distinguished economists from near and far are unified in their contention that the Pacific Rim—including nations such as China, South Korea, Japan, and Hong Kong—represents an awesome market for U.S. goods and services in the years ahead. Situated on the shores of the Pacific Ocean, San Francisco and the entire Bay Area are in perfect position to reap rewards from this trade bonanza.

As is the case with the formation of most metropolitan centers, the Bay Area developed upward, downward, and outward from an urban hub—San Francisco.

Just as they did with other frontiers in America, boat and train travel opened up new horizons for San Franciscans and set in motion the emergence of what would eventually be dubbed the Bay Area. Before there was either a Bay Bridge or Golden Gate Bridge, city folk relied on ferries and other aquatic carriers to get them to counties like Alameda and Marin where they could set off by train for day trips or vacations to popular, rural hamlets. The railroads enabled people to cheaply and easily reach such places as the Russian River country of Sonoma County and the state capital at Sacramento. Timetables preserved from the 1930s and earlier chronicle how trains of those eras made stops at tiny towns and villages that exist today only in the memories of senior citizens.

The opening of the Bay Bridge and the Caldecott Tunnel more than 50 years ago opened up then-very-agrarian Contra Costa to tourism and other types of businesses. The natural features of the county—including Mount Diablo, the Carquinez Straits, the valleys of the central county, and the tributaries of the historic Delta—were enjoyed by increasing numbers of people from throughout Northern California.

Beginning in the early 1900s, Oakland and San Jose developed as formidable urban centers in their own right. Contra Costa—then like now—benefited from its proximity to these bustling municipalities. The spill-over of commerce and population from the big cities was inevitable. Outlying counties such as San Mateo, Santa Clara, Marin, Alameda, and Contra Costa expanded at their own pace, each one nurturing economic activity that was right for its particular situation.

Two regional transportation enhancements unfolding over the last few decades were major reasons for the quick evolution of this county into highly acclaimed suburbia. Improvements to the freeway network in the Bay Area and the start-up of Bay Area Rapid Transit fueled the population boom in Contra Costa.

Also helping to foster vigorous growth was the availability of relatively affordable housing and land. With the cost of living sharply lower than in many Bay Area counties, there was nothing to hold Contra Costa back from becoming a collection of bedroom communities for San Francisco.

It should not be surprising that this burgeoning county experienced a surge in home-grown services to accommodate spiraling residential and working populations. Supermarkets, restaurants, pharmacies, cleaners, and other retail and service providers tailored their specialties to the needs of mobile, sophisticated customers.

When contrasted to other Bay Area counties whose economies can pretty well be summed up in

*Above, right: Fog rolls into San Francisco Bay, engulfing the Golden Gate Bridge. Photo by Jordan Coonrad*

*Right: Colorfully detailed Victorian homes recall memories of days past, lending a sense of history to the now modern metropolis of San Francisco. Photos by Norman Prince*

simple terms, defining Contra Costa's economy is much more complex.

Sonoma and Napa counties are noted for their agricultural endeavors; Alameda and Solano, for light industry; Santa Clara and San Mateo, for high technology; and Marin and San Francisco, for white-collar complexes. All eight have fared well in these specialized pursuits.

Contra Costa is an envied conglomeration of all of the above plus heavy industry and service businesses. The dynamism of the county's private sector can be linked to variety. The region has been able to hold on to its blue-collar roots, albeit in diminished quantity, while opening up new realms of rewarding opportunity.

Beneficiaries of this successful effort at diversifying Contra Costa business have been people from throughout the Bay Area and beyond who have obtained meaningful, long-term employment within Contra Costa's boundaries.

The strategic location of Contra Costa, with its relative closeness to all the other Bay Area counties, guarantees that this will be a place of feverish activity which faces mounting challenges in the arena of transportation.

Even with its brilliant track record of creating significant new employment, the county economy cannot

be expected to furnish enough jobs for its skyrocketing residential populace. Surely there will always exist packed trains of BART commuters en route to mostly white-collar positions in San Francisco.

Public works planners from the county and its cities can be expected during the next few decades to be fully consumed by the question of how to better move county residents to workplaces in and outside Contra Costa. The continued prevalence of lower-cost housing in outlying areas away from key employment centers will tax such freeways as 680, 242, and 4 to the limit.

Despite contrary beliefs expressed in some quarters, the land available for residential construction in this county is finite. The truth of that premise came clearly to the fore in Concord-Pleasant Hill-Walnut Creek as home and lot sizes became considerably smaller in the 1980s. In the central and south county, condominiums and single-family homes emerged on hillsides formerly reserved for cattle grazing.

The dwindling of developable property in communities like San Ramon, Pittsburg, and Martinez will prompt many future first-time home buyers to scout out adjoining counties in order to make that initial purchase. Conversely, people living in this county will increasingly be lured to new (for them) employment fron-

*Oakland has persevered as the center of activity in Alameda County, gradually gaining its own sense of strength and identity as it throws off the mantle of nearby San Francisco. Courtesy, Oakland Convention & Visitors Bureau*

*The famous Transamerica Pyramid, overlooking the San Francisco Bay, seems to grow as it reaches into the blue sky. Photo by Lee Foster*

dustrial city caught in the huge shadow of San Francisco.

Encouraging to private- and public-sector leaders in Alameda County has been the rather slow but steady renaissance of downtown Oakland. Handsome mid- and high-rise office buildings have been an uplifting influence on the senior city. Construction of a sprawling (Hyatt) Hotel and Convention Center symbolized the grand old town's aggressive attempt to get into the tourist business in a big way.

Oakland city and chamber of commerce officials have tried to recruit new business to their docks. Increased patronage of the Port of Oakland by international shipping firms holds the promise of helping to spark an eventual boom for Richmond's port as the maritime industry further embraces the East Bay.

The cultural, educational, and recreational assets of Oakland—even with the departure of the National Football League's Raiders—are substantial. There can be no denying that Contra Costa gains considerable luster from being situated near such a storied city.

Even with the dramatic growth of cities in Contra Costa and its own county, Oakland can be counted on to remain the most populous East Bay municipality for decades to come. Together with neighboring Berkeley, it forms a very important cultural and educational center made vibrant by the blending of people of many ethnic and racial backgrounds.

As starting point and terminus for Amtrak rail service in the Bay Area and home to an ever-expanding commercial airport, Oakland plays a crucial role in moving Contra Costans to destinations throughout the country.

The stately city has, for the most part, been bypassed by the relocation of large corporate operations from San Francisco to this county. Its gradual renaissance as a commercial center need not necessarily be viewed as a negative for Contra Costa.

Alameda County and this county complement each other. Because of geographic linkage, the two regions are one in the sense of offering their combined populations a myriad of goods and services within relatively easy reach.

Important events impacting an individual county's economy inevitably have a ripple effect on neighboring regions. The prosperity of the East Bay and the resultant attractiveness to builders and commercial real estate firms is the sum of business activity occurring in both Alameda and Contra Costa counties.

The interconnection between these two private sectors is perhaps best exemplified by the dramatic commercial developments that sprouted in both counties during the 1980s. San Ramon's Bishop Ranch in Contra Costa and Pleasanton's Hacienda Park in nearby Alameda County glistened with huge, relocated office complexes of household-name San Francisco corporations. The feverish leasing activity in both mammoth busi-

tiers. Stepped up commercial activity in Solano and Napa could spur the directive "Go north, young man" for many Contra Costans seeking work.

The nurturing of new high-technology and manufacturing enterprises in San Mateo and Santa Clara counties will motivate a substantial number of county residents to check out employment prospects in the South Bay. Brisk residential development in the San Ramon Valley over the last 15 years has created a deeper labor pool for peninsula employers in search of experienced, college-educated professionals—the kind of individuals in plentiful supply in Contra Costa. San Jose, among the fastest-growing big cities in the nation, is less than 30 miles from the south county.

Socioeconomic changes enveloping neighboring Alameda County are somewhat similar to what has occurred here. Oakland, the hub of Alameda, has aggressively pursued diversity of its economy, seeking to shed its widely held reputation for being primarily an in-

ness parks combined to generate national media attention.

Revitalization of commercial districts in Hayward and Fremont and the enlargement of residential areas in Dublin and Livermore are certain to make Alameda County figure even more prominently in the Contra Costa progress story during the years ahead. The availability of jobs and housing near this county's borders, as typified by the aforementioned scenarios, will sustain economic expansion by accommodating overflow demand.

In this place and time, Contra Costa is at a critical crossroads. The breakneck commercial construction that took over central county in the 1970s and 1980s is history, never to be duplicated with the

same kind of fervor. The rest of this century will be a time for cities like Concord and Walnut Creek to refine their economic structures. According to county administrator Philip Batchelor, office vacancy rates will dwindle as a new wave of white-collar corporations relocate operations from San Francisco.

"Pressure is again mounting within large companies to look toward Contra Costa as the place to transfer various office groups," Batchelor said. Increasing commute problems and rising costs of doing business in the City make it inevitable that we will be getting many more of those kinds of users.

"You will see heightened commercial building activity in the eastern and western sections of the county. As the years go by, Contra Costa will further enhance

*Above: Among the many activities and sights to be experienced in Oakland, the Jack London Village is popular spot for tourists and residents alike. Photo by Anke Van Aardenne*

*Above, left: The expansion of international shipping interests at the Port of Oakland, as pictured here by this docked Japanese freighter, assures continuing growth for the entire East Bay area. Photo by Lee Foster*

*Above: The moon rises over Mount Diablo in Contra Costa, bathing the town of Walnut Creek with soft evening light. Photo by Roc DeWilde*

*Facing page, top: Loading docks hum with activity as evening settles over the Port of Oakland. Photo by Jordan Coonrad*

*Right: The successful blending of old and new architectural styles in Oakland is illustrated by the reflection of city hall in the windows of a modern high rise. Courtesy, Oakland Convention & Visitors Bureau*

its own reputation for quality development. We will always be helped by the proximity to San Francisco and all that city stands for. Yet, at the same time, we will learn to stand taller on our own merits," Batchelor added.

Angelo Siracusa, president of the Bay Area Council, a nonprofit group primarily involved with regional economic issues, thinks that Contra Costa will continue to be a center of job creation in the Bay Area reflecting the national phenomenon of suburbanization.

"I don't see the county becoming a Silicon Valley or the like and basing its economy on the success of one or two types of industry," Siracusa said. "Diversity is what makes Contra Costa prosper. The region still has the opportunity to design its business sector in a manner that mitigates the negative aspects of modern-day living. At some point in the not-too-distant future, there will be a relative balance to the jobs/housing ratio of the county. The east county holds the key to how fast that will happen."

Hing Wong, a regional planner for the Association of Bay Area Governments, realizes Contra Costa will always rely on San Francisco in terms of providing employment for at least some of its residents. "But the reverse of that is coming true, also," he said. "San Francisco people are taking jobs here in ever-growing numbers. This county is emerging as a formidable economic center in its own right."

The years ahead for Contra Costa hold infinite promise. Leaders in the private and public sectors are joining forces to ensure that the county realizes its tremendous potential. As good as the past and present have been, the best is yet to come.

# PART TWO

# CONTRA COSTA'S ENTERPRISE

*Finance, insurance, and real es-*
*tate are among the service-*
*oriented businessess beginning*
*to flourish in Contra Costa's econ-*
*omy. Photo by Bob Rowan/*
*Progressive Image*

# CHAPTER 10

Pacific Gas & Electric, 116-117

Central Contra Costa Transit Authority, 118-119

Lesher Communications, 120-121

**Photo by Bob Rowan**

KKIS AM/FM, 122-123

Diablo Magazine, 124-125

Contra Costa Water District, 126-127

East Bay Municipal Utility District, 128-129

Concord TV Cable, 130

# Networks:

Contra Costa County's energy, communication, and transportation providers keep products, information, and power circulating inside and outside the area.

# Pacific Gas & Electric

Roughly 15 miles east of the Carquinez Strait, the giant PG&E electricity generators in Pittsburg turn out enough power for 2 million Californians. Working day and night, this power plant spins a product that moves in a blink of an eye to the homes, stores, schools, and businesses of Contra Costa County.

At the same time a 1,400-mile gas pipeline system ending in PG&E's Antioch facility brings natural gas all the way from Alberta, Canada, and distributes it to power plants, industries, businesses, and homes throughout the county.

Though most people take their gas and electricity for granted, the capacity to deliver these "invisible servants" safely, efficiently, and economically requires a vast network of dedicated employees and reliable equipment—backed up by more than a century of technological progress and innovation.

The electric part of PG&E's story began in 1879—the same year Thomas Edison invented the incandescent light. That year the California Electric Light Company, a PG&E ancestor, offered the nation's first commercial electric service in San Francisco.

Contra Costa and PG&E formed their first partnership in 1901, when they participated in what was called by a trade journal, "the greatest electrical engineering triumph ever accomplished"—a new hydroelectric power transmission system covering 142 miles between the Colgate Powerhouse on the Yuba River and Oakland. Built

*The new PG&E Learning Center in San Ramon trains hundreds of employees for a wide range of technical and administrative positions.*

by the Bay Cities Power Company, another PG&E ancestor, this system included an aerial cable crossing over the Carquinez Strait that was nearly one mile long—three times longer than any span previously attempted.

This great advance in hydroelectric power proved to be the crucial link in the electrification of the entire Bay Area and ushered in a new era of industrial productivity for the county, as Standard Oil, Redwood Manufacturers Company, Columbia Steel, and Pioneer Rubber all soon started operations in Contra Costa.

PG&E was officially incorporated in 1905. As the utility companies of the period and their customers recognized that joining systems would result in improved service and economy, many utility companies began to consolidate, and PG&E grew steadily by acquisition and merger through the 1930s.

When California's population began to

soar after World War II, PG&E launched the Contra Costa Power Plant in Antioch, the largest steam-electric plant west of the Mississippi at the time of its completion in 1951. PG&E's Pittsburg Power Plant went online in 1954 and has been expanded several times since then. Today the plant's 2-million-kilowatt capacity makes it one of the world's largest thermal electric power generating plants. Together the two plants can produce up to 3.2 million kilowatts of electricity—some 25 percent of PG&E's total generating capacity.

Gas has also played an important role in the county's industrial development. The first gas service was introduced in the county in 1914 from a PG&E Pittsburg plant, which transmitted manufactured gas to Martinez, Concord, and Antioch via an extensive gas main system. In 1930 PG&E and Standard Oil built a new pipeline from a newly discovered natural gas field in the San Joaquin Valley. From then on county customers could receive natural gas from several fields in California, and later from as far away as Texas, New Mexico, and Canada.

Today PG&E is the nation's largest investor-owned electric and gas utility. Electric service is provided to 4 million customers and natural gas to more than 3.2 million customers throughout Northern and Central California.

In Contra Costa, PG&E provides the elec-

*A PG&E gas crew tests the pressure on a gas service line as part of the company's major program to replace aging gas pipes.*

The one-mile aerial crossing the Carquinez Strait—the longest crossing in PG&E history—was completed in 1985.

tricity and natural gas to Contra Costa's 740,000 residents through two division offices: the Diablo Division, based in Concord and responsible for serving customers in central and eastern Contra Costa, and the Bay Division, based in Richmond and responsible for service to customers in western Contra Costa County and northern Alameda County. Additional offices are located in Antioch, Walnut Creek, Pittsburg, and Martinez.

PG&E maintains 2,910 miles of gas distribution lines and 86 miles of gas transmission pipe, and 3,825 miles of electric distribution lines and 539 miles of electric transmission lines in the county.

PG&E also purchases electricity from more than 1,000 wind turbines near the town of Byron. Another 1,100 wind turbines have been approved for other sites in the county. The company operates four gas and electric service centers and 30 electric substations in Contra Costa County.

The Department of Engineering Research, a 100,000-square-foot laboratory and office facility in Danville, houses 280 PG&E scientists, engineers, technicians, and administrative personnel who help guide the firm to a successful future while sustaining reliable, safe, and cost-effective operations. Many are involved in scientific evaluation, environmental studies, testing and monitoring, and general problem solving in the laboratory and throughout PG&E's 94,000-square-mile service area. Others are dedicated to research and development work on new systems, processes, procedures, or products

useful to PG&E's gas and electric operations, engineering, and planning.

PG&E's new Learning Center in San Ramon is one of the most advanced in the nation. Opened in 1987, the center includes classrooms, workshops, laboratories, conference rooms, and other facilities to train some 10,000 employees per year in courses ranging from management to maintenance, from organization planning to power plant operation.

Though the huge PG&E power plants and vast network of power cables and pipelines are impressive, it is the company's 1,900 employees in the county who are the real "invisible servants" in the PG&E story. The majority of these employees work in the Diablo and Bay Division offices, service centers, and at the power plants in Antioch and Pittsburg. Substantial numbers are also employed at the PG&E Department of Engineering Research and the corporation's new Learning Center in San Ramon, or are assigned to the Pipeline Operations or General Construction departments.

PG&E offices and plants have become one of the nation's largest industries. The company's huge investment in Contra Costa resulted in recent property taxes of $15.6 million.

Contra Costa owes much of its business and industrial growth to the electric and gas energy made available by PG&E and its ancestors. Likewise, PG&E owes much of its success to the county's population and business growth. As Contra Costa continues to grow, the Diablo and Bay divisions will continue to provide the kind of reliable gas and electric service to which the county has become accustomed over almost a century.

On the Sacramento River the Pittsburg Power Plant, one of the world's largest, generates enought power for 2 million Californians.

# Central Contra Costa Transit Authority

The Highway 24-680 Interchange, Highway 4, Ygnacio Valley Road—everyone who lives or works in central Contra Costa County knows about traffic problems. In survey after survey, county residents cite transportation as the number-one problem facing the region.

What some may not realize is that the situation could get a lot worse. Recent studies project that by the year 2000 traffic will increase 155 percent along 680 during the morning commute hours; traffic on Ygnacio Valley Road will double during peak periods; and on Highway 24—always congested in peak periods—cars will back up from the Caldecott Tunnel all the way to Walnut Creek.

Though highway improvement projects may accommodate this growth, many of these projects will not be completed in time. Some will not even begin due to lack of state funds. Creative solutions to the traffic problems are needed on every level.

Many traffic experts believe that public transportation, such as the Central Contra Costa Transit Authority (CCCTA), is one of those solutions. Popularly known as the

*The administration and maintenance building for the Central Contra Costa Transit Authority.*

County Connection, the CCCTA has initiated several innovative transportation programs to relieve traffic congestion. Its custom express bus routes, for example, take employees directly to their company locations from selected BART stations. County Connection shuttle services circulate in downtown areas, providing an inexpensive alternative to parking hassles and parking lot expense.

The residential and business communities are taking notice. Total passenger boardings have increased from 2.5 million in 1982 to 3.8 million in 1987—a 50-percent increase. Pacific Bell has contracted with the County Connection to provide express bus service from Lafayette BART to the com-

*The County Connection board of directors. In the back row (from left) are Beverly Lane, Town of Danville; Robert Schroder, Contra Costa County; June Bulman, City of Concord; Al Dessayer, Town of Moraga; Gayle Uilkema, City of Lafayette; and Charles Feyh, City of Martinez. In the front row (from left) are Carolyn Bovat, City of Clayton; Diane Schinnerer, chairman, City of San Ramon; William Dabel, vice-chairman, City of Orinda; Gail Murray, secretary, City of Walnut Creek; and John Mulhall, City of Pleasant Hill.*

pany's facility in San Ramon. Reynolds & Brown, a development firm, contracts with the CCCTA to run express service from Concord BART to Airport Plaza.

*County Connection buses provide service to 10 communities and the unincorporated area of Central Contra Costa County.*

Established in 1980, the CCCTA replaced a collection of local bus services operated by the City of Walnut Creek and by AC Transit in Concord, Lafayette, Pleasant Hill, and Moraga. From 12 small buses in 1981, the CCCTA has expanded to a fleet of 103 buses today. The number of buses operating during peak commute hours has doubled—from 39 in 1982 to 79 today. Currently the County Connection serves a 200-square-mile area from Martinez to San Ramon and from Orinda to Clayton.

The system's 24 routes run six days a week. Bus service is coordinated with BART schedules—80 to 90 percent of bus arrivals and departures at BART stations are coordinated within three to 10 minutes of train arrivals and departures.

Buses have been upgraded for comfort, appearance, reliability, and safety. Air-conditioning and two-way radio systems have been installed on all routes; all buses are equipped with wheelchair lifts; and additional passenger shelters will be built in the next few years.

County Connection drivers are the best in the business, going through an extensive job-specific training program lasting six weeks. All transit operators are instructed in emergency procedures and fire safety, and must perform daily preoperation inspections of their vehicles.

The County Connection buses and personnel recently acquired a new home—a 17,526-square-foot administration and maintenance complex on Arnold Industrial Way in Concord that was completed in 1986. The $11-million facility, jointly funded by the U.S. Department of Transportation and the State of California, contains the most up-to-date mechanical and electronic repair and maintenance equipment.

Across from the Walnut Creek BART, the County Connection Transportation Center, also opened in 1986, provides a centralized, walk-in location to serve public transit riders. The storefront center offers timetables, discount rider and commuter cards, BART passes, a lost-and-found center, and information on other Bay Area transit operators.

Governed by a board of directors composed of locally elected officials of communities within the service area, the CCCTA is the financially healthiest transit system in the Bay Area, according to a recent report published by the Metropolitan Transportation Commission. The board works closely with a citizens' advisory committee, transportation committees, and city councils on transit and transportation matters.

For the future, the County Connection has developed a strategic plan that looks beyond traditional fixed routes to alternative types of service. Subscription bus service, for example, would eliminate a great deal of highway traffic by providing long-distance commute service to high-density employment sites. Riders would board the bus at a central pickup point, such as a park-and-ride lot, and be taken virtually to their office door. Neighborhood feeder services would use jitneys in quiet residential areas to connect with the system's larger bus routes.

The CCCTA has already taken steps to increase its fleet to 111 buses by 1990 and to 150 by the year 2000. It also plans to augment its peak-period service from 79 to 90 buses and expand its hours of operation by 16 percent.

Because solving the county's future traffic problems will require nothing less than the commitment of the entire community, the County Connection is conducting an ongoing search for businesses, local governments, public agencies, developers, and employers who want to explore new ways to relieve traffic congestion. For the Central Contra Costa Transit Authority this should be easy; after all, it has had a lot of experience in making connections.

*County Connection buses serve five BART stations in central Contra Costa County.*

# Lesher Communications

Dean Lesher might never be described as having his head in the clouds, but that's just where Lesher Communications had its start.

The year was 1947, and Lesher had just learned that a small weekly newspaper in Walnut Creek was up for sale. At the time Lesher owned the *Sun-Star* in Merced but was looking to buy another paper in a vital area that could grow along with his publication. With a population of only 2,000, Walnut Creek was a small, agricultural community—known more for its walnut groves than for its growth potential—so Lesher hopped aboard a small plane to get a better view.

From the air he could see the tremendous possibilities for Walnut Creek and the entire Contra Costa County area—the roads that would someday evolve into freeways and link the area to Oakland and San Francisco, and the lush rolling hills and flatlands that would someday make a perfect setting for new residential neighborhoods.

He decided to buy the paper. Today Walnut Creek is a bustling city of 63,000 and the center of the most talked-about commercial growth story in Northern California. The small weekly has grown into the

*Contra Costa Times*, one of the most successful suburban daily newspapers in the country and the flagship publication of Lesher Communications, whose 26 publications reach more than 450,000 families in seven Northern California counties.

A native of Maryland and a graduate of Harvard Law School, Lesher's interest in the newspaper business began in the late 1930s in Kansas City, where he represented several newspapers in his law practice. He purchased his first newspaper, the *Daily Tribune*, in Fremont, Nebraska, in 1938. A few years later, unable to buck the trends of a declining market, he decided to seek opportunity in the West. He purchased his first California paper—the Merced *Sun-Star*—in 1941. Six years later the stage was set for Lesher's prophetic airplane ride over the wilds of Contra Costa.

Today Lesher Communications publishes four morning daily newspapers that cover the Contra Costa area: the *Contra Costa Times*, operating out of Lesher's Walnut Creek headquarters; the *Valley Times*, with offices in Pleasanton; the *San Ramon Valley Times* with offices in Danville; and the *West County Times*, with offices located in Pinole. These papers are supported by two weeklies: the *Contra Costa Sun*, keyed into the Lafayette, Moraga, and Orinda area, and the *Concord Transcript*, serving the county's larg-

*Dean Lesher, publisher.*

est city.

Covering the east Contra Costa area are the *Antioch Daily Ledger* and the *Pittsburg Post Dispatch*, both afternoon dailies, and the weekly *Brentwood News*.

In addition, Lesher publishes three specialty publications—*New Horizons*, for senior citizens; *Real Estate Review*, for home buyers; and *Your Guide To . . .*, for new residents.

*Lesher Communications' headquarters in Walnut Creek.*

*A satellite receiving dish for transmission of the* **New York Times.** *The national edition is printed at Lesher Communications.*

---

Four other Northern California counties—Solano, Marin, Sonoma, and Napa—are served by Lesher weekly newspapers and shopping guides. Lesher recently acquired a newspaper in Placer County, the *Roseville Press-Tribune.*

Eight Lesher publications are produced in the firm's Walnut Creek headquarters in the Shadelands Office Park, the site of the old Shadelands Ranch off Ygnacio Valley Road. A 200,000-square-foot office and production facility, the plant is one of the most modern in Northern California, incorporating the latest publishing technology. Top-of-the-line press and laser-scan color-separation equipment provide the award-winning color for which Lesher publications are renowned.

The company's computerized typesetting technology allows Lesher artists to design all types and sizes of ads at a single console and send them to laser typesetting machines. The firm's satellite dish receives Associated Press transmissions that can be called up directly on editors' VDT screens. In addition, the plant can receive AP photos via dedicated phone lines in eight minutes and print them in color.

This kind of high-quality production capability enabled Lesher Communications to become the fourth regional printing site for the national edition of the *New York Times* in 1984.

Awards for editorial, advertising, production, and overall newspaper excellence are

---

*The 16-unit Goss Metro offset press used to print Lesher Communications' dailies.*

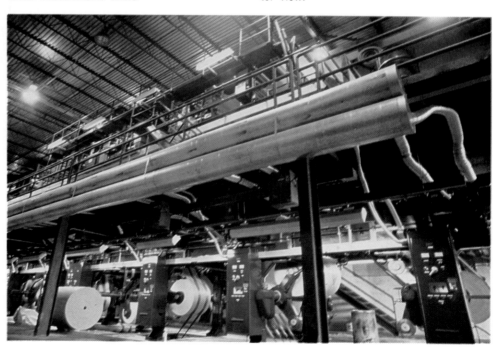

an annual tradition for the *Contra Costa Times* and many other Lesher publications. In 1979 the *Times* was named the Best Daily Newspaper in the state by the California Newspaper Publishers Association. Dean Lesher was named Publisher of the Year in California by the California Press Association in 1977, and received the Suburban Newspapers of America first annual Dean S. Lesher Award in 1982. The following year the National Newspaper Association's highest award for distinguished leadership in the newspaper industry was presented to Lesher by President Ronald Reagan in ceremonies at the White House.

Over the years Lesher's personal involvement with civic and community organizations has served as a forceful catalyst for business and community development in the Contra Costa area. His generous donations to charitable organizations, hospitals, and scholarship funds has helped to shape the future of the community. As just one example, the innovative Communications Career Training Program in Walnut Creek, introducing high school students to the world of newspaper publishing with real hands-on experience, has proved to be one of the most popular programs among high school students in the area.

A good newspaper can be a strong force for progressive change in a community, and this philosophy has guided Lesher Communications throughout its history. The company is dedicated to playing an active role in the future development and quality of life in Contra Costa County. As it turned out, a short plane ride more than 40 years ago has given all Contra Costa residents a better view.

# KKIS AM/FM

Over the past two decades Contra Costa County has evolved from an outlying Bay Area suburb into a thriving business and residential community—with its own unique identity, life-style, as well as media. One of these homegrown media is KKIS radio—Contra Costa's only combined AM-FM station.

KKIS (990 AM and 92.1 FM) broadcasts a wide range of music programming as well as news, regular traffic updates, weather reports, and a full lineup of community-oriented programs, all with a distinct Contra Costa perspective.

"Sure, many people here want to know about events and activities in San Francisco," says Jim Chabin, president and general manager of KKIS, "but they really want to know about local traffic, weather, and activities in Contra Costa because they live here, not in San Francisco. The city stations can't and won't focus on the county like we do."

KKIS-AM first went on the air in 1949, one of the many radio stations to be licensed in the postwar era. At that time the county consisted of a group of fairly small farming areas, and KKIS was more of a community medium than an entertainment vehicle: If a cow got lost somewhere in Antioch, for example, the urgent message was broadcast on KKIS.

In the 1960s and 1970s, however, Contra Costa became an affluent suburb, with a fast-growing population and an even faster-growing per-capita income. Local and national advertisers began to recognize this dynamic consumer base—and realized that they could reach it with KKIS.

The station experienced steady growth along with the rest of the county throughout the 1970s. In 1983 Chabin, western marketing manager for CBS Television stations in Los Angeles, was determined to purchase a radio station. Though a great deal of his experience was in television, he had been fascinated by radio since his high school days in Kansas.

"I wanted to buy a radio station very badly," Chabin recalls. "But it had to be the right station, in the right area. After looking at different stations all across the country, we chose these two."

Chabin changed the call letters of the station to KDFM and the station's program format from "beautiful music" to adult contemporary. The station's three studio locations in Pittsburg, Walnut Creek, and Concord were combined into one new modern headquar-

*More than 4,000 people attended the KKIS California Balloon Race, a fund-raiser for Special Olympics.*

ters at 1975 Diamond Boulevard in Concord. Over the next five years the station's staff more than doubled and now employs 25 on-air personalities, technicians, salespeople, and administrative personnel.

Today, in many significant ways, KKIS has returned to its roots as a community information medium. As part of its community focus, KKIS provides public affairs broadcast time to a number of civic groups, such as the "Council Commentary" program produced by the Contra Costa Council. In addition, KKIS co-sponsors Contra Costa USA, a major business-outlook conference and exposition that has featured such noted speakers as former President Gerald

R. Ford, ABC News correspondents Sam Donaldson and Howard K. Smith, and Los Angeles Mayor Tom Bradley.

Another reason for KKIS' appeal in Contra Costa is the technical nature of radio broadcasting in the Bay Area. In addition, FM radio signals cannot be heard at all from Sacramento and can only be picked up with great difficulty from San Francisco, due to the surrounding mountainous terrain. KKIS-FM is the only commer-

*Above: Former President Gerald Ford addresses Contra Costa USA 1988, sponsored by KKIS and the Contra Costa Council.*

*Left: Kaufman and Broad vice-president Debra Bernard (left) and KKIS president Jim Chabin (right) present a new home to KKIS listener Dawn Stiles during the KKIS Dream Home Giveaway.*

tion has also made it a breeding ground of radio talent—many KKIS employees have gone on to further their careers in San Francisco and other larger markets.

KKIS, broadcasting 24 hours per day, 365 days per year, celebrates its 40th birthday in 1989. With more than 125,000 loyal listeners per week, KKIS has truly become the Voice of Contra Costa.

cial FM station licensed in Contra Costa County and delivers a strong stereo signal throughout the county.

Though KKIS does not try to imitate the San Francisco stations, their proximity has inspired the station to provide the best programming possible.

"Contra Costa is no longer a small suburban community," says Chabin. "We have sophisticated listeners who are used to hearing the best, so our goals have to be higher than if we were a more isolated community. Though we don't consider the San Francisco stations to be our competition, we must put out a product that is just as good."

As a result, more than 200 local and national advertisers use KKIS to reach the Contra Costa market. The quality of the sta-

*ABC News White House correspondent Sam Donaldson speaks to attendees at Contra Costa USA 1987.*

# Diablo Magazine

Where can you find a hard-hitting look at the future of Contra Costa business, a guide to the best golf courses in the East Bay, and a review of Mexican restaurants in the area—all in the same publication? The answer is *Diablo*, the only magazine geared to the unique tastes, issues, and needs of Contra Costa County.

Since its founding 10 years ago as a small newsprint tabloid, *Diablo* has evolved into a sleek, full-color regional monthly, with a circulation base of more than 50,000. The magazine's readership was substantially increased in April 1988, when it began full newsstand distribution throughout Contra Costa County, Alameda County, and San Francisco.

The brains behind this publishing success story belong to Steven Rivera, who left his director of marketing position at the *Chicago Tribune* to start the magazine in 1979. Naming the magazine *Diablo Country*, Rivera focused on life-style topics that matched the rural-suburban profile of the community at that time.

"Our readers loved the magazine almost from the start," says Rivera, "because it gave them a sense of community, an identity that other publications were not providing."

As Contra Costa began to evolve into a cosmopolitan business/financial center, the editorial content of the publication became more sophisticated. In June 1986 the publication added "Magazine of the East Bay" to the cover, and in January 1987 the word "Country" was dropped from the title.

Though *Diablo* was obviously expanding its horizon, the magazine still refused to abandon its interest in the small-town aspects of the community. It will continue doing stories about farms where readers can pick pumpkins and stables where they can rent horses. *Diablo* still relishes the rural quality of the area.

Publisher Rivera emphasizes the magazine's close ties with the county. "In many ways, *Diablo* is a mirror of Contra Costa County," he says. "As the county has offered more and more in terms of commerce and culture, *Diablo* has been able to offer more, to reflect the county's enhanced quality of life. In a sense, *Diablo* is a watchdog for that quality of life."

The metaphor is apt: Over the years the magazine has watched the area's health care services, child care facilities, and business practices, as well as the latest restaurants, retail stores, and entertainment events, advising readers on the best in East Bay products and services.

In addition, *Diablo* provides a rich mixture of feature articles on topics ranging from community trends in fashion, cuisine, recreation, and travel to in-depth profiles of well-known business and community leaders, Bay Area sports figures, and entrepreneurs who provide that rare valuable service few people know about.

*Diablo* is more than light life-style fare. In recent years the magazine has also run timely investigative news stories on such topics as drug dealing in Contra Costa schools, racism in the East Bay, and taken a look at the effects of divorce on children.

*Steven Rivera, founder of* Diablo *magazine.*

Many of these articles, written by nationally known writers, have garnered praise and awards from professional journalistic organizations.

"To be a true voice of the community," says Rivera, "we have to show the county the way it really is by publishing an honest, well-rounded picture. That means covering problems faced by the community. This doesn't detract from the quality of life—just the opposite: Through understanding these issues more completely, we can improve the quality of life here."

The magazine has also sought

to improve the community in other ways—by supporting and sponsoring many charitable and community events, such as the Devil Mountain Run benefit for Children's Hospital; Contra Costa USA, the annual business outlook conference; and most recently, the Contra Costa Hall of Fame Awards.

The one-man operation in 1979 has expanded to 35 full-time employees in 1988. The magazine's staff not only performs editorial, administrative, and advertising functions, but also its own in-house production of the magazine.

As the circulation of *Diablo* has increased, so has the magazine's advertisers. Many Contra Costa companies, institutions, organizations, and retail outlets have recognized that they can convey their message to a targeted Contra Costa readership.

In October 1987 *Diablo* moved to new offices at 2520 Camino Diablo in Walnut Creek. An adjacent building will accommodate staff growth in the future years—growth that is virtually assured if Contra Costa continues at anywhere near its present growth rate.

Though *Diablo* magazine now has wider coverage, more timely stories, and a more sophisticated graphic look, it probably won't change a great deal in the years ahead. "Our features and departments have always served the community," says Steven Rivera. "That hasn't changed and never will."

*Diablo* **magazine serves as a "true voice of the community" and features articles on such varied topics as fashion, travel, cuisine, and in-depth profiles and examinations of community leaders and current affairs relating to the community.**

# Contra Costa Water District

Contra Costa County has changed dramatically over the past 50 years, and so has its water supply requirements. The county's population has increased by more than 70,000 people since 1980, with the most rapid growth occurring in the north-central and eastern areas—the areas served by the Contra Costa Water District.

The district currently provides treated water to 195,000 people in Concord, Clayton, Pacheco, Vine Hill, and portions of Walnut Creek, Martinez, and Pleasant Hill. Another 142,000 in Antioch, Pittsburg, West Pittsburg, Martinez, and Oakley are served by cities and water utilities that purchase CCWD's untreated water from the Contra Costa Canal and treat it themselves.

CCWD was created in 1936 to ensure a reliable water supply for the county. At that time agricultural irrigation was reducing the water flow through the Sacramento-San Joaquin Delta, allowing saltwater from San Francisco Bay to intrude into the region. A typhoid outbreak in Pittsburg had also raised fears about water quality.

In the early 1930s a group of citizens led by attorney Thomas Carlson lobbied the federal government for passage of the Central Valley Project Act, which included construction of the Contra Costa Canal, a 52-mile-long channel from Rock Slough in the delta to Martinez. The federal government committed to the Central Valley Project in 1937, and the CCWD—which was formed by Contra

*Contra Costa Water District's flocculation basins (foreground) and sedimentation basins at the Bollman Water Treatment Plant in Concord.*

Costa voters in 1936—was assigned to contract, purchase, and distribute the water provided by the U.S. Bureau of Reclamation. The Contra Costa Canal, delayed by World War II, was completed in 1948, though the first water from the canal was delivered to the city of Pittsburg in 1940.

For its first 25 years the CCWD purchased and distributed untreated canal water; the cities and water utilities within the district were responsible for treating water used by their customers. However, in the late 1950s many citizens and public officials became concerned about the quality and cost of water in the central county area. To solve the problem CCWD purchased the California Water Service Company's Concord area treatment, pumping, storage, and distribution facilities and entered the treated water business.

Since that time the CCWD has achieved a worldwide reputation for innovation and technological advancement in water treatment. When the Bollman Water Treatment Plant was completed in 1968, it was hailed as state of the art by water treatment technologists. Patents on two treatment processes held by the district are used at water treatment facilities worldwide as part of the district's commitment to improving water quality.

Maintaining a reliable supply of high-quality water is an ongoing concern for the CCWD. When rainfall and Sierra snowfall

*Above: CCWD's Contra Loma Reservoir is located in Antioch. It holds a three-day emergency supply for more than 350,000 customers.*

*Left: CCWD's Contra Loma Reservoir. The reservoir for the City of Antioch is in the background.*

CCWD's sedimentation basins at the Bollman Water Treatment Plant in Concord. Treated water is distributed to 195,000 customers in Central Contra Costa County.

are sparse, supplies of high-quality water become strained. There is less freshwater to hold back the saltwater of San Francisco Bay, and the quality of delta water deteriorates. But quality isn't the only problem. Currently the district has only a three-day emergency supply of water in its Contra Loma Reservoir, compared to the 180-day supply of the East Bay Municipal Utility District and the 260-day supply of the city of San Francisco.

After extensive study the district's board of directors recently proposed the construction of Los Vaqueros Reservoir as the best solution to the dual problems of quality and reliability. A large reservoir to be built in the Kellogg watershed of eastern Contra Costa County, Los Vaqueros would allow CCWD to store high-quality delta winter flows and purchase Sierra water during

wet years for blending with delta water in dry seasons. It would allow the CCWD to better meet water quality needs and provide six months of emergency storage.

To protect the reservoir water, CCWD is negotiating land purchase use over the entire Los Vaqueros watershed area.

Other benefits of Los Vaqueros would include flood control, a potential for energy generation, and possibly recreation. Within carefully planned environmental guidelines, the shores of the reservoir could provide areas for picnicking, hiking, and other activities.

On November 8, 1988, sixty-eight percent of CCWD voters approved funding for Los Vaqueros. Construction will begin on the project in the early 1990s and could be completed by 1995.

The district's longtime commitment to the community is demonstrated in its strategic placement of treated water storage reservoirs. Many have been placed underground and landscaped to blend in with the surrounding terrain. Some underground reservoirs, such as Paso Nogal Reservoir in Pleasant Hill and Bailey Reservoir in Concord, have been integrated into the local recreational facilities. More than 15 miles of bicycling

and hiking trails have been developed along the Contra Costa Canal. The district board also offers its meeting rooms at no charge to community and nonprofit groups.

Along with its quest for higher-quality water, CCWD runs several ongoing programs geared to conserving its product. The district regularly distributes conservation tips to customers and has sponsored numerous conservation conferences for landscape architects, large water users, and home owners. In addition, a new pilot Comprehensive Residential Water Audit Program was conducted to prepare county residents for future water shortages.

For more than 30 years CCWD has conducted an extensive canal safety education campaign that reaches more than 25,000 youngsters annually. Water education workshops and classroom materials on the origin of the water supply are provided to Contra Costa teachers. More than 1,000 students tour the Bollman plant each spring, and hundreds of others hear classroom presentations on water treatment. In conjunction with the Mt. Diablo Unified School District, CCWD co-funds the R.V. Crago, a converted World War II landing craft that takes students on water environmental studies expedi-

The delta provides the water for CCWD's 350,000 customers.

tions into the delta.

The Contra Costa Water District sees water as a precious resource that must be planned for well into the future. In Contra Costa, growth and dry weather are inevitable—and so is the need to provide the water resources that will accommodate both conditions.

# East Bay Municipal Utility District

Water is a resource often taken for granted: People assume that water will always be available when they turn on a faucet. However, recent droughts remind one that nothing should be taken for granted—especially the water one needs to live.

Contra Costa's water is supplied jointly by two agencies: the East Bay Municipal Utility District (EBMUD) and the Contra Costa Water District. EBMUD supplies water to 20 cities and 15 towns in Alameda County, and west and central Contra Costa County, including Walnut Creek, Lafayette, Richmond, and San Ramon. The Contra Costa Water District serves most of the remainder of the county.

EBMUD was created in 1923 when the people of Alameda and Contra Costa counties voted to establish the district to provide a safe, plentiful regional water supply. The district's directors searched far beyond local sources, which were deficient in either quantity or quality. Instead, they chose to import water from the High Sierra watershed of the Mokelumne River.

Every spring, melting snow cascades down the Sierra Nevada mountains into the river, which flows to Pardee Dam and Reservoir near the town of Jackson. Built in 1929 in a narrow rock canyon, EBMUD's main water collection reservoir is 345 feet high and holds more than 68 billion gallons of water—almost a year's supply for the East Bay.

From Pardee Reservoir the water travels through three parallel aqueducts another 90 miles to the East Bay, where it is stored in one of five large terminal reservoirs—Briones, San Pablo, Lafayette, Upper San Leandro, and Chabot.

The decision to use the Mokelumne River watershed has resulted in one of the world's safest drinking water systems. A major 1983 study showed EBMUD's water to have the lowest level of mineralization of any Bay Area source. EBMUD now collects, stores, treats, and delivers this precious resource to more than 1.1 million customers.

The Mokelumne River decision also illustrates that the selection of today's drinking water must be made with tomorrow's standards in mind. The district's present estimated safe water yield is approximately 240 million gallons per day (MGD), and current use stands at about 218 MGD. Though this may seem like plenty of cushion, projections show that district water needs will exceed the current supply by the year 2000—less than 12 years from now. Severe droughts, such as the current one and that of 1976-1977, also jeopardize the adequacy of the water supply.

In order to meet future East Bay needs for more high-quality drinking water, EBMUD signed a contract with the federal government in 1970 to purchase water from the American River, which has water quality comparable to the Mokelumne. However, a lawsuit filed in 1972 by environmental groups and the County of Sacramento has stalled the project for nearly 17 years.

While the case has been in litigation,

*The watershed of the Mokelumne River provides pure snowmelt from the Sierra Nevada to serve a population of 1.1 million East Bay residents.*

EBMUD is considering a Water Supply Management Program to manage and improve the water system, meet future demands, and assure delivery in case of system failures, such as earthquakes or flood damage to the aqueducts. The program proposes expansion of conservation and reclamation projects, building new terminal reservoir storage, strengthening aqueducts that cross unstable Delta islands, and purchasing rights-of-way for a fourth aqueduct.

Today EBMUD encompasses a vast system of reservoirs, watershed lands, treatment plants, and distribution facilities. A powerhouse at the base of the Pardee Dam generates approximately 110 million kilowatt hours of electricity each normal water year, enough power to meet the needs of a city about the size of Danville. The electrical power, which is sold to Pacific Gas & Electric, provides energy to Californians and income for EBMUD to help keep water rates low for customers.

The district's 42,000 acres of watershed lands are maintained to protect the water that runs into the reservoirs. In 1986 EBMUD purchased 469 acres of land in the Briones watershed to improve water quality protection. The purchase eliminates the possi-

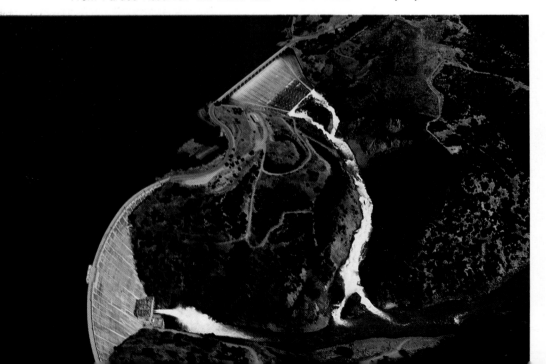

*Pardee Dam, completed in 1929, impounds 68.4 billion gallons of water at full capacity.*

bility of housing development and accompanying pollution within the watershed.

Some of the district's lands and reservoirs are also used for recreation. The Lafayette Reservoir, for example, may be used for picnicking, hiking, sailboating, canoeing, and rowboating. Gasoline boats, swimming, waterskiing, or other water contact activities are not permitted.

Water treatment is one of the agency's most important tasks. To remove any remaining dirt, algae, and bacteria, the district's water is purified at six treatment plants. Chemical tests performed at the plants and at 53 other points in the system assure that health standards are met. EBMUD also adds fluoride as a dental benefit and lime to reduce acid that may cause damage to its pipes and customers' plumbing.

Distribution to customers is a complex process. Water is sent through more than 3,600 miles of pipe, 120 pumping plants, and 162 distribution tanks and reservoirs. More than half of all water supplied by EBMUD goes to homes for outdoor and indoor use. The remainder is used by business and industry for various purposes.

Water supply was EBMUD's only business in its early years, but as rapid growth and inadequate sewers began to contaminate San Francisco Bay, six East Bay cities turned to the agency to solve the problem. A plant was built to treat wastewater from homes and industries and to discharge treated effluent to the Bay. Since EBMUD's first treatment plant began operation in 1951, water quality has improved, odors along the shoreline have disappeared, and bay water recreation has flourished. EBMUD now treats wastewater for nearly 600,000 people.

Recently EBMUD instituted a number of new improvements to upgrade water quality and service. In 1987 the district in-

*Briones Reservoir, one of five reservoirs in the East Bay hills, is higher in elevation than Pardee Reservoir in the Sierra foothills. Thus, its water can be routed wherever it is needed within the distribution area.*

stalled a new high-technology operating network called OP/NET, which provides a central control center to manage distribution operations and maintains water quality at highest levels. OP/NET also allows the district to take better advantage of off-peak energy rates and improves reliability of service for thousands of Contra Costa customers.

Water conservation is another important part of EBMUD's overall water quality program. The district's Urban Water Management Plan, initiated in 1986, is expected to trim 18 MGD from the water demand projected over the next 20 years. Elements of the plan include conferences for landscape professionals about water-saving techniques, drought-resistant landscaping requirements in new annexations, free consultations to customers on ways to conserve water, and distribution of special low-flow showerheads and

toilet dams. EBMUD also has an ongoing conservation program of reusing highly treated wastewater for nondrinking purposes.

EBMUD is also participating in a number of projects vital to water distribution and treatment in Contra Costa. In San Ramon, major new pipeline systems, three medium-size reservoirs, and three new pumping plants were completed to meet the needs created by population and building booms. A major overhaul of the Orinda filter plant was completed in 1988.

As the quest for clean water is not limited by institutional boundaries, the district cooperates with the Contra Costa Water District and other agencies to assure a high-quality water supply for the entire region. A new contract with CCWD will provide surplus water to the new Los Vaqueros reservoir if approved by CCWD voters in 1988. EBMUD's Key Contact program, launched in 1985, keeps EBMUD officials up to date on the needs and concerns of communities in Contra Costa.

EBMUD employees are continually working to determine the district's water needs and availability. Teams of hydrographers survey the snowpack to calculate how much water will be available for the coming year. Demographic analysts project population growth to predict the need for future water supply and equipment. EBMUD's Project WATER regularly supplies Contra Costa classrooms with educational materials on water conservation.

When water is treated as a precious, finite resource, looking to the future becomes a way of life. It has been that way for East Bay Municipal Utility District for more than 60 years, and will continue far beyond tomorrow.

*Sobrante Filter Plant is one of the six modern treatment facilities ensuring that water of the highest-possible quality is delivered to EBMUD customers.*

# Concord TV Cable

Cable television has been one of the nation's fastest-growing industries over the past 20 years, and Concord TV Cable is no exception to this general trend. The City of Concord first awarded the cable franchise to the company in 1967, and subsequent awards were made by the City of Clayton and by Contra Costa County. By the end of its first year of operation the firm had connected 2,000 subscribers and today serves more than 40,000 subscribers.

Over the years Concord TV Cable has built a strong reputation for customer service, picture quality, and a wide range of programming. Originally building a 12-channel system, the company rebuilt to add eight more channels in 1982 and another 18 in 1984. It now offers 38 channels and plans to add four more before the end of 1989.

Current subscribers to the basic service receive 14 Bay Area and Sacramento broadcast stations, 14 satellite-delivered services, and a local public-service (access) channel. Cable FM connections deliver more than 30 radio services, many of which are not receivable with a local antenna. Premium Service subscribers choose from a

*This satellite earth station, located east of Alberta Road, provides Concord TV Cable viewers with crystal clear reception. Photo by D. Schroeder*

wide array of movie and entertainment programming—HBO, Showtime, The Movie Channel, Disney, and Playboy—and individual pay-per-view movies and major sports events, such as GiantsVision and championship boxing matches.

In 1967 Concord TV Cable had 11 employees; today it employs 73 in its administration, sales, engineering, installation, customer service, computer, and warehousing departments. A new facility at 2450 Whitman Road features 22,000 square feet of of-

fice and warehouse space, an expansive lobby, ample off-street parking, and room for future growth.

The antenna site on Lime Ridge near Mt. Diablo and the satellite earth station east of Alberta Road deliver their signals to subscribers through a cable distribution network of nearly 400 miles. Full-service standby power capability, to be completed in 1989 and 1990, will keep the entire system operating during power blackouts.

Owned by Walnut Creek based Western Communications, Inc. (WesCom), a subsidiary of Chronicle Publishing Company, Concord TV Cable is a leader in the Contra Costa community and in the cable industry. The original president, Court Kirkeeng, and current president, Ernie Nelligan, have been continuously active on the boards of many local civic organizations.

With many new and planned improvements—a new antenna tower for better local reception, the new building, extended office and telephone hours, additional channel capacity, 100-percent standby power, and senior citizen discounts—Concord TV Cable marches into the future with the adopted motto, "If better is possible, good is not enough."

*CTVC's new headquarters on Whitman Road provides 22,000 square feet of office and warehouse space and ample off-street parking. Photo by D. Schroeder*

SAN FRANCISCO
DALY CITY

165

15
5
C 1

BART
ba

Photo by Mark E. Gibson

# CHAPTER 11

Photo by Jordan Coonrad

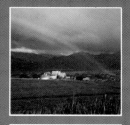

California and Hawaiian Sugar Company, 134

Jacuzzi Whirlpool Bath, 135

Micropump Corporation, 136-137

Dow Chemical U.S.A., 138-141

# Manufacturing:

**P**roducing goods for individuals and industry, manufacturing firms provide employment for many Contra Costa County area residents.

# California and Hawaiian Sugar Company

Many Contra Costa firms have known the sweet smell of success, but the California and Hawaiian Sugar Company (C&H) knows the true meaning of the expression. It is one of the nation's largest marketers of sugar, producing one million tons of sugar and 300,000 tons of molasses per year.

C&H was founded in 1906 when Hawaiian sugarcane growers banded together to combat fluctuating prices and increased competition on the U.S. mainland. By forming C&H the growers could sell their sugar under a single label and compete with other U.S. refineries on an even basis.

That same year the C&H refinery in Crockett began to process the sugarcane shipped from Hawaii. Once the largest flour mill on the West Coast, the Crockett refinery provided 500 new jobs for the small San Pablo Bay town and over the years has been the economic anchor for the community.

In 1921 C&H became a tax-exempt agricultural processing and marketing cooperative. Today the firm is owned by Hawaii's 13 sugar companies and 265 independent

*A typical Hawaiian sugar mill in a cane field, the source of all C&H sugar.*

sugar growers—all of which own proportionate shares of the organization. After all shipping, refining, and selling costs have been met, the remaining revenues are returned to the growers.

Sugar has long been Hawaii's most important agricultural product: Approximately 26,000 jobs in Hawaii are created by growing and processing Hawaiian sugarcane, and hundreds of other jobs are provided on the mainland in refining, selling, and distributing Hawaii's sugar.

The sugarcane is milled in Hawaii and turned into raw sugar, a light brown product that resembles large-grained sand. The

*The C&H refinery on the Carquinez Straits of San Francisco Bay, where ships from Hawaii unload their cargo.*

raw sugar is loaded on one of C&H's specially designed ships for the five-day trip to San Francisco Bay, where it is refined and packaged.

With 10 floors of high-speed equipment—enough to cover 20 football fields—C&H's Crockett plant is the largest sugar refinery in the world. More than 800 people are employed at the facility, many of them the third generation of employees who started in the refinery's early days.

More than 100 different kinds and package sizes of refined sugars are processed at the plant. These include a wide variety of packaged sugars for consumers, as well as a full line of liquid, brown, and granulated sugars for industrial use. The refinery also has storage facilities for approximately 55,000 tons of packaged, bulk, and liquid sugars.

After C&H sugar is refined and packaged in Crockett, it is shipped by trucks, railcars, and vans for eventual distribution across the United States, though predominantly west of the Mississippi.

In addition to the Crockett refinery, the company's facilities include a smaller refinery near Honolulu, new headquarters in Concord, and several sales, distribution, and storage centers scattered throughout the western states. The new C&H Concord headquarters opened in July 1987 at 1390 Willow Pass Road and employs 100 people.

With its two major facilities in Contra Costa, C&H will continue to sweeten the life of the county for years to come.

# Jacuzzi Whirlpool Bath

Getting people in hot water is not usually a sound strategy for success—unless, of course, your name is Jacuzzi. Over the past few decades the Jacuzzi name has become as familiar as Coca-Cola and Xerox, and Jacuzzi Whirlpool Bath, headquartered in Walnut Creek, has become the leader of the home whirlpool bath and spa industry.

The company offers approximately 25 whirlpool bath designs and 14 spa designs in a variety of shapes and sizes. Many use microchips, sensors, touch-sensitive controls, and fully integrated electronic systems. The firm's products have become so influential that they are now a standard amenity in new home construction.

Jacuzzi was started in 1915, when the seven Jacuzzi brothers immigrated to Berkeley from a small town near Venice, Italy. After the brothers developed a pitched propeller and landed a contract supplying the government's World War I effort, the success of the venture allowed the move of the rest of the family—six sisters, mother, and father—from Italy to America.

After the war the business produced fans, furnaces, and wind machines that protected fruit orchards from frost. In 1926 the family developed a water-injection jet pump that would be the forerunner of their highly successful whirlpool bath.

Over the next two decades the family business expanded with jet pumps of various sizes, designs, and capabilities. As California grew wealthier and more prosperous in the 1950s, the company added a line of pool equipment. When one of the original brothers needed a way to provide hydrotherapy at home for his arthritic son, the organization fashioned a portable pump that whipped up air and water in an ordinary bathtub.

Though hospitals and athletic groups found soothing comfort in the portable whirlpool pump, it remained mainly a medical and institutional product through the 1960s. It was in 1968 that Roy Jacuzzi, a third-generation member of the family, invented the home-use whirlpool bath that would make the company's biggest splash. The new product incorporated and concealed all the jets, pumps, and motors, and the public took to the concept immediately.

Since that time the firm has continued to introduce new industry firsts: totally assembled plug-in spas, a complete service program such as those for appliances, long-term warranties, and a full line of mass-produced whirlpool baths developed for builders.

Today Jacuzzi Inc. is a part of the New York-based Hanson Industries. The company employs roughly 2,200 people worldwide (500 in California), and has seven manufacturing plants throughout the world.

While the residential market is the major sector of Jacuzzi's growth, the company's products are also used widely in hospitals, hotels, and health clubs. With its innovative past, the firm seems certain to become the wave of the future in many types of settings.

*Below: Roy Jacuzzi, president and chief executive officer of Jacuzzi Inc.*

*Bottom: The Aura™ by Jacuzzi Whirlpool Bath.*

# Micropump Corporation

What do X-ray machines, racing cars, and ink jet printers all have in common? They all use a precision magnetic-drive gear pump developed by the Micropump Corporation of Concord.

The company's products may be unfamiliar to the layperson, but they are integral components of technologies used in almost every area of daily life. Water is purified with equipment that contains Micropump technology. Farmers use Micropump equipment to grow crops. Cardboard boxes, direct-mail pieces, and other media are printed with ink jet technology that relies on Micropump technology. Research laboratories and manufacturing plants worldwide depend on Micropump technology to produce medicines, chemicals, automobile cooling systems, even spacecraft.

As with many important inventions in this century, the pump was developed in a garage—this one was located in Danville

and belonged to Thomas B. Martin. The year was 1960, and Martin had just left his research engineer position at General Electric Corporation in San Ramon to develop some ideas of his own. A number of his inventions had been patented, and he had helped develop General Electric's turbo fan and other engines.

One of Martin's ideas was a magnetic coupling that would greatly increase the efficiency and life of small gear pumps by eliminating both leakage and friction of packing rings. After developing the coupling, Martin was joined by Pete Pieters, a skilled machinist who built the first pumps, and Robert W. Leonard, a marketing professional who sold Micropump's initial products to industry.

Among the venture's first customers were the airlines, which used the devices in aircraft galleys to pump water into coffee makers. At one time every major airline used the pumps. Today they are used in a wide range of industries and settings: research and development laboratories, medical instrumentation, electronics, chemical and pharmaceutical plants, food processing, and transportation.

From a fledgling company Micropump has grown to 120 people housed in a 38,000-square-foot plant in Concord and a new branch facility near Cambridge, England, to serve the rapidly expanding European market. The firm produces 60,000 to 70,000 pumps per year in 17 standard models ranging in weight from 1.1 to 22 pounds.

Micropump has enjoyed its greatest growth since 1985, when Wayne Ross acquired controlling ownership of the corporation. Once a controller with the firm, Ross ascended to the presidency in 1983 and purchased the company from Martin two years later. Since that time Micropump has opened its Cambridge office, implemented state-of-the-art quality-control and scheduling systems, and forged partnerships with many of the world's leading manufacturers. As a result, Micropump doubled sales over

*Micropump Corporation now employs 120 people in its 38,000-square-foot plant in Concord and has just opened a new branch facility near Cambridge, England, to serve the rapidly expanding European market.*

the three-year period.

Ross recognized that the company's solid experience with Micropump technology was its major strength. More than one-third of Micropump's employees have been with the firm in excess of 10 years.

The organization has also innovated several quality-control and scheduling systems. Through its statistical quality-control (SQC) program, employees are responsible for monitoring and controlling the quality of their output, not only in production departments but also in operation, accounting, engineering, marketing, and sales. Micropump's commitment to quality is evidenced by progress charts openly displayed at work stations throughout the company. Since the implementation of the quality-control system, the firm boasts a less than .5-percent reject rate.

Micropump's Just-In-Time (JIT) scheduling system is based on customer needs rather than the customary goals or quotas set by various department managers. The company-wide system has resulted in a miniscule finished-goods inventory, minimum production and operating costs, and on-time shipment to both domestic and international customers. Through consistent JIT procedures, Micropump has maintained a near 100-percent on-time shipment record over the past two years.

Another major factor in the firm's success is its strong customer service orientation, which emphasizes long-term relationships. Toward this end Micropump provides prompt sales and engineering support, dedicated distributor support, and custom-design engineering services—establishing in effect a partnership with the customer to meet the needs of the end user. Many Micropump customers have used the company's products for more than 15 years.

The corporation's contributions to the quality of life are particularly evident in the medical and pharmaceutical industries. Every year thousands of lives are saved using hemodialysis life-support systems containing Micropump technology. The research and testing of hundreds of medicines would be complicated without magnetic-drive gear pumps.

The impact of the company's products are experienced worldwide—sometimes even far above and below it: NASA, for example, used Micropump technology in its Skylab and space shuttle craft; also, the recovery vehicles involved in the search for the *Titanic* used pumps developed by the Contra Costa firm.

In the future Micropump plans to expand into other areas of fluid systems for which its pumps are designed. A company with such a long tradition of quality, innovation, and high-powered leadership should be pumping life into the county's economy for a long time to come.

*Micropump Corporation produces 60,000 to 70,000 pumps per year in 17 standard models ranging in weight from 1.1 to 22 pounds.*

# Dow Chemical U.S.A.

In 1916, when San Francisco business baron Mortimer Fleishhacker founded a fledgling chemical company in Pittsburg, California, he hardly could have anticipated the long-lasting and beneficial impact it would have on Contra Costa County. But today, as Dow Chemical U.S.A. gets ready to celebrate its 50th anniversary at the Contra Costa site where Fleishhacker started the Great Western Electrochemical Company, there is no doubt about the far-reaching progress and development that have taken place.

Today Dow's Pittsburg plant site, headquarters of the Western Division, is the largest integrated chemical complex in the western states. Dow's research activities at the site, as well as at its Walnut Creek Center, are among the largest industrial research operations in the West. The Pittsburg site has become a respected spawning ground for some of the most talented scientists, researchers, and managers in the chemical field. Equally important, the Western Division has employed thousands of Contra Costa residents throughout its five-decade residence, contributed significantly to the local tax base, and liberally donated money, manpower, and support for cultural

and community improvement projects. Together The Dow Chemical Company and Contra Costa County have shared a unique history of dynamic growth that stretches over more than a half-century.

It all began in 1916, when Fleishhacker and a group of prominent San Francisco leaders began exploring business opportunities in Contra Costa County. Anticipating the development of the West's great industries based on agriculture, forest products, oil, and mining, the group decided to found an electrochemical company that could serve these industries.

The first move was to identify a location that offered access to water and transportation facilities. A parcel of land, located on the New York slough of the San Joaquin River between the cities of Pittsburg and Antioch, proved to be ideal. It not only offered water and transportation, but easy access to raw materials and a source of surplus power from a nearby electrical generating plant.

The plant's initial products included chlorine, caustic soda, and bleach to serve the needs of the West's forest products industries. Other products were soon added, including solvents, potassium chlorate, and hydrogenated oil. The plant's engineers even developed a way to liquefy chlorine so that it could be shipped safely.

During World War I most of the Great Western Electrochemical Company's products were commandeered for the war production ef-

fort. As soon as the war was over the company jumped back on the fast track by developing, producing, and marketing products especially designed to serve the West's mining, forestry, agriculture, and high-technology industries. The firm expanded both its product development activities and presence in the West. Sales offices were set up in San Francisco, Los Angeles, and Seattle, and regional distribution warehouses were built in Los Angeles.

Established in 1897 at Midland, Michigan, The Dow Chemical Company's initial charter was to manufacture products from salt brines. As new technologies and industries emerged, Dow began looking for strategic relationships or acquisitions that would enable it to expand its national presence. The Great Western Electrochemical Company was just such an opportunity. On January 1, 1939, The Dow Chemical Company purchased the Great Western Electrochemical

*The Great Western Electric Chemical Company—the forerunner of Dow Chemical—in the year of its founding, 1916, in Pittsburg, California.*

a much broader view. Its expanded research operations brought about developments that ultimately affected all facets of life, improving health and worker safety while safeguarding the environment.

Research developments of the 1950s included better processes to produce synthetic fibers; the first artificial kidney dialysis devices, which have since saved many, many thousands of lives; and reverse osmosis processes for water purification and for gas and liquid separation techniques, which have made it possible to engineer production plants that not only are safer and more efficient, but also are cleaner for the environment. The division's research operations also developed new ways to generate electrical energy, new pharmaceuticals and anti-cancer medicines, new and more durable plastic foam materials, and safer preservatives and coatings.

In 1953 the Western Division purchased a 54-acre site in Torrance, California, and built a plant to produce polystyrene, foam insulation and flotation materials, epoxy resins, and other products

*Left: Lacking the safety equipment standard in industry today, these 1946 workers were pleased with their efforts atop old plant 26.*

*Below: Robert McPherson and Art Swezey repot tomato plants as part of Dow's early research work at the Seal Beach Agricultural Research Division.*

Company. It was Dow's first major manufacturing expansion outside of its home base in Michigan.

The new Dow division, initially called the Great Western Division, devised a rapid expansion program to serve western needs. Early on the division placed great emphasis on research, and in 1941 established the first organized industry research facilities for agriculture, located in Seal Beach, California.

The facility focused its initial research on the problems encountered by Southern California's citrus industry. Later it expanded into virtually every facet of western agriculture. Many of the chemical tools for food production in use today were developed by this pioneering group of research scientists.

In 1951 the Western Division turned the focus of its manufacturing operation to

needed by the West's growing plastics industries. The division also established the first technical service group in the West—a group dedicated to helping the plastics industry make the best use of the growing number of complex new plastics products.

In the 1960s Dow's growth continued at a fast clip. In 1960 the Western Division established a plant in Fresno, California, to manufacture plastic film for the packaging, agriculture, construction, and consumer markets. In 1962 Dow built the Walnut Creek Research Center, and four years later the division completed construction of a unique electrical power generating plant at Pittsburg. It used modified jet engines, fueled with natural gas, to cogenerate both electric power and steam. The power-generating plant not only met all of the Pittsburg

plant's substantial needs for electric power and steam, but also was a forerunner of cogeneration plants in use throughout the West today.

The 1970s also were a time of progress and development for Dow. Two notable events stand out. First, the Western Division built a modern marine bulk liquids terminal in Long Beach, California, that featured the most advanced technology available at the time. Second, the division completed a program that effectively removed all discharges of contaminated process water to the river at its Pittsburg site. In addition, the plant modified its production processes so that less water from the river was needed for cooling. Today the plant meets all of its drinking water requirements by accessing underground wells on its prop-

erty, utilizing water purification processes developed in its research laboratories.

The Western Division's water purification developments not only were put to good use at the Pittsburg plant, but ended up serving the community as well. For example, during a severe local drought several years ago, Dow used the purification plant to supply salt-free water—free of charge—to thousands of Contra Costa residents whose health was threatened by the high salt content of public water supplies.

Over the years the Western Division has achieved much state and national recognition for its employee health and safety pro-

*Today the Pittsburg plant has one of the most modern and extensive distribution terminals in the West.*

*The campus of the Walnut Creek Center's research facilities.*

grams, as well as for its responsible and innovative environmental stewardship programs in manufacturing.

Studies have been made of all manufacturing employees who have worked for the division since the early 1940s. These studies revealed that Dow employees are healthier and live longer than the national average for the healthiest working population group.

The division employs a staff of industrial hygienists to monitor worker chemical exposures in a chemical manufacturing environment and to develop programs to assure that these exposures present no health hazards. Dow also has established a medical health center at the Pittsburg plant to constantly monitor employee health. The center sponsors a number of health maintenance programs for employees and their families.

Dow has a strong, long-term commitment to environmental safety. The Western Division maintains a substantial staff of environmental engineers and specialists. It monitors production operations and develops new and innovative ways to reduce the plant's environmental impact. In fact, Dow's highly respected environmental staff is recognized by government agencies as technical

problem-solvers capable of effectively dealing with an array of environmental issues.

In effect, the Pittsburg plant is a self-sufficient mini-city. It generates its own power, supplies its own water, offers on-site medical services to its employees, and provides its own fire, security, and environmental safety services.

While the plant may be self-sufficient, it is hardly isolated from the surrounding communities. Many of the Dow people who live and work in Contra Costa County are very involved in community service projects. The Western Division strongly encourages its employees to participate in community events and has numerous programs to bring both local and corporate recognition to employees for such activities.

In addition to being one of the county's larger taxpayers, the division also has a substantial corporate grant program designed to provide financial support for cultural and community-improvement projects. Also, Dow's investments to maintain and improve its operational facilities contribute tremendously to the economic well-being of the community.

The backbone of all Dow activities and accomplishments is the people. Presently Dow

employs approximately 850 people at its Contra Costa County locations. Many of these people have made major contributions to scientific, industrial, and community progress. In addition, the Western Division has become a rich source of senior management talent for Dow. Its graduates have become executive vice-presidents for the firm. In fact, one Western Division alumni was named chairman of the board of directors. They have also been chosen to serve as presidents of major subsidiary companies and world area operating units of Dow.

As Dow Chemical U.S.A. gets ready to mark its 50th year in Contra Costa County, there is much to celebrate. But from Dow's perspective, this half-century mark is just a beginning. Dow will continue to provide safe, high-quality jobs for the community, develop innovative products for diverse industries, and act as a launching pad for future industry leaders, scientists, and researchers so that the next 50 years will be as exciting and challenging for Dow and Contra Costa County as the past 50.

# CHAPTER 12

Photo by Dick Luria/After Image

Chevron Land and Development Company, 153

Mason-McDuffie Insurance Service, Inc., 154-155

Concord Chamber of Commerce, 156

Contra Costa Council, 157

Armstrong Lorenz Gilmour & Whalen, 158

# Business
# and
# Professions:

Greater Contra Costa County's professional community brings a wealth of service, ability, and insight to the area.

# Trembath, McCabe, Schwartz, Evans & Levy

*Synergy in action. Sharing ideas to solve problems is commonplace at Trembath-McCabe. Here lawyers and staff meet regularly to tap one another's talents. Photo by Barry Evans*

The worn leather binding of *Bennett's 1850 California Reports* can be seen reflecting off the screen of the Westlaw computer terminal in the law library of Contra Costa County's Trembath, McCabe, Schwartz, Evans & Levy, Professional Law Corporation. The firm represents a tradition of strong local presence keeping pace with the ever-changing dynamics of contemporary law.

Unprecedented commercial and urban growth have offered Contra Costa County and the "680 Corridor" an array of new opportunities. They have also brought new challenges—finding solutions to the complex legal problems that inevitably accompany growth. For more than 20 years the lawyers of Trembath-McCabe have been helping Contra Costa County businesses and families find creative and effective solutions through personal involvement and high-quality legal services.

"Our practice has been a direct reflection of the county's growth," says founder

Michael P. McCabe. "As Contra Costa County has blossomed, and many national and international companies have established offices and plants here, so has our practice expanded to meet their needs."

In 1967 founder James R. Trembath, then a San Francisco attorney, looked at his native Contra Costa County and studied its future. The Bay Area path of growth was inevitable, and the prospect of helping to shape that growth brought him home. Trembath honed his financial and real estate skills as corporate counsel to a Contra Costa County based financial institution. His practice today concentrates on the legal aspects of financing, developing, and operating both commercial and multiple-residential properties. Trembath also leads the firm's banking practice.

Trembath sees Contra Costa's great challenge as finding a balance between economic expansion and preserving the county's quality of life. "Contra Costa must maintain a community spirit," he says, "and a regional approach to preserving and enhancing the Contra Costa County life-style. That's why we live and work here."

Like Trembath, many of the firm's attorneys have chosen to move their practices from San Francisco and Oakland to the community where they live. McCabe came in 1969. His clients stretch from the wind turbines of the Altamont Pass to the wineries of Sonoma. More recently, partner James N. Dawe served as vice-president and chief legal counsel to a publicly traded international corporation before choosing to practice close to home. The firm still continues as legal counsel to the company, and Dawe may still be required to show up, on a day's notice, in Chicago, London, or cities around the Pacific Rim.

"But," says Dawe, "the advances in communications systems make it possible, for the first time, to work efficiently and effectively close to home. And the proximity of Buchanan Field makes Los Angeles literally an hour away."

Like the other attorneys, Dawe enjoys helping business people solve thorny problems: "Whether it's a lease interpretation, a questionable trademark, or a complicated financing decision, I like to help my clients make practical decisions."

Brian P. Evans, born in Boston and raised on the East Coast, was still in law

*When negotiations fail, the ultimate test is in the courtroom. Here Marchmont J. "Jim" Schwartz addresses a jury in the Contra Costa Superior Court before Judge Gary E. Strankman. Richard Lenzi is the court reporter. Photo by Barry Evans*

*Buchanan Airport is Contra Costa's doorway to the world. Here Jim Dawe visits with flight captain Carl D'Benedetto en route to a distant business negotiation. Photo by Barry Evans*

school when he started working for the firm. Hired to assist McCabe in the trial of a major civil rights lawsuit, Evans carefully researched the evolving Constitutional law and helped McCabe prevail in the court of appeals. Now an experienced trial attorney in his own right, Evans enjoys a special interest in the legal aspects of unfair business competition, trade secrets, and toxic contamination. Like other attorneys in the firm, he represents his clients' interests not only in the local courts, but in the federal courts and in the courts of other states as well.

Evans also exemplifies the firm's involvement in community affairs. He has served as president of the Contra Costa County Barristers' Association (dedicated to continuing education and improving skills among young lawyers), serves on the board of governors of the Alameda-Contra Costa Trial Lawyers Association, and serves as financial chairman of the Right Direction Project (dedicated to assisting youth struggling with contemporary problems).

"We are always willing to step up to bat for a worthwhile community cause," says Evans. "We believe that 'giving something back' contributes significantly to the communities where we live and practice—and

it broadens the perspective of the attorneys as well."

Long known for its abilities in dispute resolution, whether in negotiations, arbitration, or trial, the firm boasts a host of experienced trial lawyers. Marchmont J. "Jim" Schwartz, whose practice emphasizes real estate and business litigation, recognizes the realities of resolving disagreement. "Finding the facts, knowing the law, examining the background and motives of the witness—these are the responsibilities of the trial lawyer," says Schwartz. "But in an era when courts are crowded and the expense of litigation extreme, lawyers must find creative alternatives to trial. That requires finding out what people really want and need—and finding a way to get there. That's when lawyers are at their best."

There is a leadership quality in the law firm. It is reflected in the presence of David J. Levy, affable former president of the State Bar of California. Levy, too, came to Contra Costa from San Francisco—but in 1947. Serving as personal counselor to many of the area's leading families and as city attorney or district counsel for several Contra Costa County municipalities, Levy played a major role in the county's economic growth and development. BART, the Sunvalley Shopping Center, and the Concord Pavilion are among a few of the major projects Levy helped bring to Contra Costa. His public service continues. In 1983 he chose to affiliate with his current

partners because of the "creative vitality" of the lawyers and staff. "They were involved and they were making things happen," says Levy. "They still are. I like that."

Over the years the firm's focus on local business issues has carried over to many worthwhile community projects, such as the pro bono services it provides for a number of charitable foundations, municipal boards, and civic organizations. Whether the client is a *Fortune* 500 company or the family of an individual seriously injured in an accident, whether the issue is a wrongful employment termination or the need for a tax-saving trust, Trembath, McCabe, Schwartz, Evans & Levy has always believed in providing full service

The number of attorneys in the firm now ranges in the mid-teens, with a total staff exceeding 30. Almost all are local residents. "We are continuing to grow to meet the needs of our community," says McCabe. "When a client retains this firm, they retain the entire firm—not just a single attorney. We work better together than alone. And our clients are better served by our synergy and experience."

*Local business is the mainstream of Contra Costa's economic activity. Here Trembath-McCabe's Arlene Segal confers with shopping center manager Susan Young. Photo by Barry Evans*

# McCutchen, Doyle, Brown & Enersen

McCutchen, Doyle, Brown & Enersen is Contra Costa County's largest law firm. Founded in San Francisco in 1883, McCutchen now has more than 235 attorneys in offices in San Francisco, Walnut Creek, San Jose, Washington, D.C., Shanghai, and Taipei. Its Walnut Creek office is the product of a merger in 1985 with the regional firm of Van Voorhis & Skaggs, whose attorneys had practiced in Contra Costa since 1960. With more than 30 attorneys, the Walnut Creek office offers businesses and selected individual clients a breadth of local experience combined with the depth of business and litigation expertise of an international multi-office law firm.

The firm has demonstrated a strong commitment to community service, believing that active involvement both improves the community and builds ties that ultimately assist clients. Among the partners are former mayors of Walnut Creek and Moraga, two citizens of the year of their respective cities, the former city attorney of Walnut Creek, the current president of the board of the East Bay Municipal Utility District, and several leaders of the incorporation efforts in Orinda and Moraga. McCutchen attorneys also perform pro bono publico work for several nonprofit civic organizations, including the Kennedy-King Scholarship Foundation and the Diablo Foundation for the Aging. One partner is presently leading the effort to raise $15 million to build a regional arts center.

This local involvement is matched by a tradition of service to the legal profession. McCutchen attorneys regularly lecture and write in their areas of specialization. Lawyers in the Walnut Creek office have lectured for the American Bar Association, the Continuing Education of the Bar program, the American Law Institute, and the law

*Left: Supervisor Sunne McPeak reviews a development proposal with Dan Curtin.*

*Below: Tailoring development to the local environment is a McCutchen specialty.*

schools at Stanford, the University of California at Berkeley (Boalt Hall), and Hastings. This commitment to continuing education ensures that the attorneys are well versed in both the current law and in the trends that are shaping the future of the law.

An example of how McCutchen combines its local ties with its specialized legal expertise has been the firm's work as general counsel to the developer of the Blackhawk residential community. In the early 1970s the firm was retained to advise the Blackhawk developers on a host of complex land-use and environmental issues. For several years, the firm's attorneys worked to obtain land-use approvals and, when those approvals were challenged in the

courts, successfully defended them. Once Blackhawk's approvals were obtained, the firm drafted the covenants, conditions, and restrictions that guided development, prepared construction contracts, provided securities counseling in the sale of the country club to its membership, and gave tax advice on many aspects of the project. Blackhawk is a showcase of McCutchen's real estate practice, now one of the largest in Northern California.

McCutchen has also gained prominence in the representation of financial institutions such as the CivicBank of Commerce. Claude Hutchison, chairman of the board of CivicBank, reports, "In 1982 CivicBank was the dream of local businessmen. We wanted a local bank that would help local business. In selecting general counsel, we needed a firm that was prepared to start small with us as we raised our initial capital and then grow as we grew. McCutchen met that need." As the bank expanded, its need for capital increased. McCutchen attor-

*Above: Managing partner Sandy Skaggs confers with CivicBank board chairman Claude Hutchinson.*

*Right: Doc Merrill works with executives of Computer Task Group on a new software system.*

neys obtained the required regulatory approvals and prepared a second stock offering to provide this capital. Today, with more than $200 million in assets, Civic-Bank has branches in Oakland, Walnut Creek, and San Leandro.

These examples illustrate the range of skills, resources, and legal expertise that McCutchen offers the businesses of Contra Costa County. Responding to the needs of its varied clients, the firm provides specialists in virtually every area of law relating to business, including corporate, securities, environmental and natural resources, intellectual property, labor and employment, tax, estate planning, and trust law. Also widely known for its litigation capabilities, the firm offers experts in real prop-

erty, product liability, environmental, antitrust, securities, and general commercial litigation.

McCutchen, Doyle, Brown & Enersen is enthusiastic about the future of Contra Costa and looks forward to providing legal services and community involvement that will foster the county's continuing growth.

# Central Bank

From its roots in California's Gold Rush days, Central Bank has become one of the largest, most stable banks in the state. Headquartered in Walnut Creek, the institution offers a complete range of banking, financial, and investment services for both individual customers and businesses.

The Bank of Oroville, Central Bank's predecessor, was founded in 1892 to meet the needs of the area's growing towns and mining centers. Agriculture was replacing gold as California's most promising industry, but logging and railroading were also making contributions to the state's commerce.

Deposits in the new bank commonly took the form of gold dust, which was weighed and sent to the San Francisco Mint, where it was transformed into gold coins. Though many of the bank's depositors were miners, early customers also included surrey builders, railroad executives, politicians, dredger men, and agricultural growers and packers.

The bank has been actively involved in Contra Costa County for 40 years. In 1949 the bank opened two branch offices in the county, one in Oakley and the other in El Cerrito. In the late 1950s the institution opened offices in Orinda, and in the late 1960s acquired Concord National Bank and built a branch office at the County East Mall in Antioch.

*Today Central Bank has nine branches in the county. The county's accelerated growth, strong economy, and skilled labor pool were major factors in relocating the bank's headquarters to Walnut Creek in 1984.*

Today Central Bank has nine branches in the county, including the offices of Pittsburg's Delta Pacific Bank, which Central acquired in 1988. The county's accelerated growth, strong economy, and skilled labor pool were major factors in relocating the bank's headquarters to Walnut Creek in 1984.

Just as the Bank of Oroville was founded to serve the needs of its community, so too has Central Bank consistently developed innovative services designed to meet the needs of individuals and businesses faced with radical changes in the financial services environment.

Augmented by a sophisticated automated teller machine network and a well-trained and highly motivated employee team, Central Bank's complete range of individual banking services includes checking and savings accounts, retirement accounts, auto leasing programs, consumer loans, safe deposit boxes, travelers' checks, and insurance programs.

The bank's Consumer Services Division offers individual customers all types of consumer loans, including home improvement and home equity, auto, recreational vehicle, airplane, boat, and mobile home loans.

Businesses of all types and sizes find a flexible and comprehensive array of financial services. A commercial lending program features term loans, accounts receivable financing, and lines of credit. Services to both the residential and commercial/

industrial sectors have been marked by a history of innovative loan products. Construction loans have long been a specialty of the bank through its Real Estate Industries Group. Central also specializes in making loans to churches and other religious institutions through its Church Loan Group.

Central Bank's business equipment and automobile leasing program is expansive. Cenval Leasing, the bank's auto leasing subsidiary, has consistently developed innovative products that are used by hundreds of auto dealers in several midwestern states where Cenval operates. Central's equipment leasing subsidiary boasts floating rate leases for commercial lessees and issuance of certificates of participation for underwriters of municipal programs.

Central offers a wide assortment of financial and accounting services, such as computerized payroll, tax reporting, general ledger, and order processing; collection and disbursement services; and information and reporting services. Many new and established Contra Costa businesses have taken advantage of this cost-effective means for handling complex accounting functions.

Coast Program, Central Bank's insurance premium finance division, is California's largest lender of funds for the purchase of personal lines of auto insurance. This division recently developed an insurance underwriting rating system that is marketed to insurance agents, insurance companies, and managing general agents through-

*Headquartered in Walnut Creek, Central Bank offers a complete range of banking, financial, and investment services for individuals and businesses.*

out California, Texas, Arizona, New Mexico, and Nevada. In addition, the division recently implemented an on-line document management system to eliminate paper storage, the first of its type in California.

Both corporate and individual customers can choose from a wide array of investment products offered by Central's Capital Markets Group: U.S. Treasury Securities, mortgage-backed securities (such as Ginnie Maes), tax-exempt municipal securities, tax-deferred annuities, money market instruments, and many more.

In the Contra Costa communities where Central has branches, the bank is active in chamber of commerce events and other civic activities. Each year the bank actively promotes the Contra Costa Chapter of the March of Dimes and the TeamWalk fund raiser. Concerned about traffic issues, the bank is a member of the Contra Costa Centre Association.

With its quality loan portfolios and its proven ability to innovate new products and services, Central Bank will continue to progress toward its centennial anniversary. The bank views Contra Costa County as a major market area and the perfect hub for its elaborate network of branches and statewide operations.

# Thiessen, Gagen & McCoy

Today a law firm must offer highly specialized legal services on a cost-effective basis in order to survive and grow. This is especially true in Contra Costa County, where businesses are starting up or expanding almost daily and demand a wide spectrum of legal expertise to handle new ventures and projects.

Since its founding in 1965, Thiessen, Gagen & McCoy has evolved into one of the leading law firms in the county by meeting these needs. The growth of the practice from two to more than 25 attorneys is testimony to its reputation for integrity, leadership, and community service.

Today Thiessen, Gagen & McCoy counsels and represents numerous banking institutions, private and publicly held corporations, hospitals, major developers, community groups, general and limited partnerships, and individual entrepreneurs—not only in Contra Costa, but also across the state of California as well.

The firm offers a broad array of legal services for both businesses and individuals. For business clients Thiessen, Gagen & McCoy provides legal services in real estate development, land use, zoning, contract interpretation, and litigation; banking, insurance, business formation, acquisition, and dissolution; labor relations; and tax planning.

For individual clients Thiessen, Gagen & McCoy offers services in family law, estate planning and probate, personal injury, criminal, and juvenile law.

Recognized statewide for its estate planning and probate knowledge, Thiessen, Gagen & McCoy attorneys have authored parts of legal publications used as reference texts by the California State Bar. In this field the firm handles all phases of will and trust preparation and counsels clients on minimization of income, death taxes, and avoidance of probate.

Thiessen, Gagen & McCoy has long been known for its special expertise in criminal, family law, and juvenile law matters. With a state bar-certified criminal law specialist and also a certified family law specialist on staff, the firm offers skilled counsel in all segments of these practice areas.

Over the years the firm has gained a reputation for excellence in trial practice, with broad experience in civil, personal injury, family law, and criminal litigation. Its attorneys practice in all federal and state courts, including the United States Supreme Court, United States Court of Claims, and the United States Tax Court.

Thiessen, Gagen & McCoy employs an experienced and well-trained staff, uses the most advanced computer and word-processing technology, and maintains a comprehensive law library that features computerized legal research services.

The firm's partners—Brian D. Thiessen, William E. Gagen, Jr., Gregory L. McCoy, Patrick J. McMahon, Mark L. Armstrong, Linn K. Coombs, and Stephen W. Thomas—live in Contra Costa County and have strong roots in the community. The firm provides active leadership in community, charitable, civic, church, and cultural organizations. Its members coach youth sports and participate in chamber of commerce activities, area-wide foundations, Boy Scouts and Girl Scouts, the YMCA, and local community centers.

The members also serve the legal profession through various bar associations, serving as faculty at local universities and in elected and appointed positions in government—adding a dimension of experience that extends beyond the normal confines of a law office. Two former members of Thiessen, Gagen & McCoy are currently judges in Contra Costa County Superior Court.

*Left: Brian D. Thiessen*

*Center: William E. Gagen, Jr.*

*Right: Gregory L. McCoy*

*The Thiessen, Gagen & McCoy law offices at 279*
*Front Street in Danville. ©Chris Scott*

# Arthur Young & Company

As a Big Eight accounting firm, Arthur Young & Company has long provided tax and consulting services to some of the nation's largest corporations. In January 1986 Arthur Young relocated its Oakland office to the Tishman Center in Walnut Creek to serve the growing needs of Contra Costa County and the entire Bay Area.

The Walnut Creek practice offers full-service accounting and consulting support for a broad range of clients, and specializes in two major areas: health care and emerging middle-market entrepreneurial companies, two of the fastest-growing segments in the county.

For providers of health care services, Arthur Young's full-service approach encompasses a wide range of expertise: strategic and financial planning to facilitate mergers and acquisitions; financial feasibility studies for renovation, expansion, and acquisition projects; analysis and implementation of medical and financial information systems; development of productivity and staffing standards; review of medical records operations to document and enhance patient care; management of cash flow and investments and development of banking relationships; and

*Pictured here are three of the five partners in the Walnut Creek office of Arthur Young & Company. Shown (from left) are Jim Karling, Jim Gorman, and Jerry Engel.*

design and implementation of new systems of health care delivery.

The firm currently serves more than 100 health care organizations in Northern California, including hospitals, long-term care facilities, HMOs, PPOs, and medical groups, many of which are located in Contra Costa County.

Over the years Arthur Young has gained a reputation as the Big Eight firm in high technology, a focus exemplified by the Walnut Creek office. The company's Entrepreneurial Services Group (ESG) is a unique practice among the Big Eight firms, designed to work with owner-managers and decision makers to provide financial and business ser-

*The Walnut Creek practice of Arthur Young & Company offers full-service accounting and consulting support for a broad range of clients, and specializes in health care and emerging middle-market entrepreneurial companies. Here are two Arthur Young & Company partners, Mark Pickup (left) and Jerry Bajada, who work with these clients.*

vices for startup, high-growth, and closely held businesses. As these businesses grow into international firms, ESG provides increasingly complex financial and consulting services to meet their needs.

Bay Area ESG clients include major companies in the biotech/biomed, computer, semiconductor, software, telecommunications, and aerospace high-technology industry segments. The ESG practice also specializes in the retail, real estate, and construction industries.

The five partners in the Walnut Creek office—James Karling, partner-in-charge; Jerry Engel, director of the Entrepreneurial Services Group; James Gorman; Mark Pickup; and Jerry Bajada—bring years of professional experience in a wide array of areas. In addition to their professional achievements, the partners are also active leaders in the community, serving as board members for several local service and civic organizations.

For the future, the partners of Arthur Young & Company envision expansion of their Walnut Creek facilities to accommodate personnel increases beyond the 100 employees currently working at that location. As the needs of Contra Costa's business community become more demanding, the practice will expand to meet those needs.

# Chevron Land and Development Company

Some real estate ventures become so large and successful that they take on the stature of incorporated communities. In Contra Costa, Blackhawk and Bishop Ranch spring to mind and so does Hilltop, a complete urban center containing more than 3 million square feet of retail, office, industrial, and residential space.

Probably best known for its 120-acre Hilltop Mall—one of the largest shopping centers in the Bay Area—the entire Hilltop development spreads across 950 acres just off Route 80 in Richmond.

Hilltop was developed by Chevron Land and Development Company (CL&D), a subsidiary of Chevron Corporation. CL&D started as a relatively minor diversification activity in 1965 when three employees of Standard Oil (now Chevron) were reassigned to oversee the surplus land that Chevron had acquired over the years. Their assignment was to look into ways of developing, liquidating, or otherwise disposing of lands no longer needed for the company's petroleum operations. Four years later, when the Hilltop project was created, CL&D was no longer a minor diversion.

Today, nearly 25 years after its modest beginnings, CL&D has 90 full-time em-

*Adjacent to Interstate 80, with Mount Tamalpais in the background, the Hilltop development combines commercial and residential buildings, recreation and office space, and research and development facilities over 950 acres in Richmond. Photo by Baron Wolman*

ployees who manage more than one billion dollars in assets. Those assets include office buildings, retail projects, industrial parks, and mixed-use projects.

The organization's major projects range from the 5,000-acre Coto de Caza master-planned residential/resort community in Orange County to high-rise office buildings in Denver and New Orleans. To date the company and its affiliate, Huntington Beach Company, have participated in the construction and sale of 3,000-plus homes, primarily in Southern California. More than 10,000 residential units are planned for CL&D's current inventory of land.

Hilltop, the jewel in CL&D's Northern California crown, is now a flourishing community, combining commercial and residential, recreation and office space, research and development, and office development. The community includes a wide choice of residential housing, with more to come. Hilltop Vil-

lages boasts more than 500 luxury condominiums and single-family homes. Hilltop Bayview offers garden apartment living, featuring swimming pools, tennis courts, and electronic security. Hilltop West, which borders the Richmond Country Club, will provide a mix of housing, with commercial services for residents and Bay views.

Hilltop Mall is home to Macy's, Emporium-Capwell, JCPenney, and 120 specialty stores. Day-care facilities, restaurants, supermarkets, banks, and theaters are all conveniently located within the Hilltop development. A new 150-room full-service hotel features banquet rooms, conference facilities, restaurant, and lounge.

Hilltop's location, access to major transportation, and amenities have made it extremely attractive to relocating businesses and corporations. Over the years the development has emerged as a center for scientific and biological research and development companies that appreciate the proximity to UC Berkeley. A recent Hilltop development includes two Class A office buildings, part of the eventual one million square feet of office space called for in Hilltop's master plan.

With its prime location, design excellence, and attention to sensitive planning issues, Hilltop is exemplary of Chevron Land and Development Company's projects and will continue to be an important force in the county in the coming decades.

*Plaza Two, one of the Class A office buildings in the Hilltop development office park.*

# Mason-McDuffie Insurance Service, Inc.

The past decade has witnessed many changes in the insurance industry. Claims and jury awards have skyrocketed, forcing many insurers to raise premiums. Some industries and groups have found it difficult to obtain certain types of coverage. The insurance industry itself has had to withstand several periods of soft-market conditions.

At the same time the insurance needs of Contra Costa County have changed: Once almost strictly a personal insurance market, the county now has a broad-based business population as well.

Mason-McDuffie Insurance Service, Inc. (MMIS), headquartered in Pleasant Hill, has taken this roller coaster ride to become one of the nation's largest privately owned insurance brokerage firms. MMIS currently provides tailored insurance programs to more than 25,000 business and individual clients in Contra Costa and throughout the state of California.

"A major trend in the insurance industry has been the tendency of smaller agents to disappear or band together," says president and chief executive officer Jay O'Brien. "We've managed to stay indepen-

*Mason-McDuffie Insurance Service, Inc., represents many major insurance companies, including Hartford, Transamerica, American States, Chubb, Commercial Union, and Fireman's Fund, to name just a few. Through its Association Division the firm designs tailored programs for all types of organizations, associations, and groups.*

dent and so can provide faster, more individualized service at lower rates."

One measure of the agency's success is its rapid growth and loyal clientele. From 1982 to 1988 its premium volume has more than quadrupled, increasing from $7 million to more than $27 million. Many of the firm's clients have been insured with MMIS for decades.

As a well-established and respected broker, MMIS represents many major insurance companies, including American States, Chubb, Commercial Union, Fireman's Fund, Hartford, Ohio Casualty, Safeco, Transamerica, and United Pacific.

Through its Association Division the

*Mason-McDuffie Insurance Service, Inc., headquartered in Pleasant Hill, has become one of the nation's largest privately owned insurance brokerage firms.*

firm designs tailored programs for all types of organizations, associations, and groups. All types of policies are handled, including combinations of fire insurance on buildings and businesses, property, business liability, professional liability, and group workers' compensation.

For many years the company has been one of the nation's leading insurance specialists for the pet care industry—veterinarians, veterinary hospitals, kennels, groomers, and other pet industry specialists. MMIS has developed special group packages and safety programs for more than 1,500 veterinarians and pet care professionals statewide.

Mason-McDuffie also designs insurance programs for boat owners: The company's Marine Division, known as Trans-Pak Insurance Agency, is the largest insurer of private pleasure craft in California, with more than 13,000 clients.

Though its focus is primarily business coverages, Mason-McDuffie also provides a wide range of coverages for individuals, families, and commercial enterprises: home owners', health, life, automobile, renters', aircraft, and condominium insurance, as well as popular "umbrella" liability policies.

Mason-McDuffie Insurance was founded in Berkeley, California, in 1887 as

part of Mason-McDuffie Co., one of the nation's largest privately held mortgage banking and real estate companies. O'Brien joined the firm in 1965, after a seven-year tenure with Northern Insurance in San Francisco. He became a general partner in 1972. Ten years later, when the five divisions of Mason-McDuffie reorganized into separate companies, O'Brien took over the leadership of the newly formed Mason-McDuffie Insurance Service.

functions, but also runs an insurance evaluation program that determines the best coverage and rates for clients on an individual basis.

One of the major reasons for the firm's success has been its talented, dedicated personnel. Many Mason-McDuffie brokers and agents have more than 25 years of experience assessing clients' needs and determining the best coverage for them. Many are well known in the insurance indus-

try, holding leadership positions in such professional associations as Professional Insurance Agents Association of California, Western Association of Insurance Brokers, and California Association of Insurance Agents. All MMIS brokers and customer service representatives attend continuing education programs that enable them to stay current on the latest developments in this complex, rapidly changing industry.

Perhaps the single most important factor in the firm's success is service. "We work extremely hard at service, especially individualized service, and we pay a lot of attention to clients' risk management needs," says O'Brien.

The company's customer service representatives handle inquiries, update records, and renew and revise policies quickly and accurately. In many cases small claims are handled through Mason-McDuffie rather than the insurer so that clients receive personal, efficient service from the agency that designed and sold the coverage.

With a century-long tradition of service, Mason-McDuffie Insurance Service, Inc., has the ability to tailor insurance programs to the specific needs of Contra Costa businesses and residents. As the county continues to grow and change, the service will undoubtedly include many alterations.

*Two views of the exterior of the Mason-McDuffie Insurance Service, Inc., headquarters.*

Donald Hook began his career with the Kemper Group in 1953. He joined Mason-McDuffie in 1970 and became a full partner six years later. In 1982 Hook became executive vice-president of MMIS and the head of the agency's Southern California operation in Santa Ana.

In 1985 Mason-McDuffie acquired Trans-Pak Insurance Agency, which is now run as MMIS' Marine Division, headed by former Trans-Pak owner Gary Swiggett. In recent years the company has acquired several smaller insurance agencies, which have been integrated into Mason-McDuffie's operations. On September 5, 1988, Mason-McDuffie became a wholly owned subsidiary of Transamerica Insurance Group.

Today MMIS employs 79 people in its Pleasant Hill headquarters and in offices in Santa Ana, California, and Seattle, Washington. All MMIS offices are fully automated to provide fast, efficient service and personal attention. The company's mainframe computer not only generates policies and premium notices and maintains all accounting

# Concord Chamber of Commerce

For more than a half-century the Concord Chamber of Commerce has been a major factor in the business growth of Contra Costa County.

Though the chamber is business oriented, it tries to enhance the quality of life for all community segments. "We want to create the right atmosphere for planned growth," says Harry York, executive vice-president. "We try to make sure that our decisions are right for the entire community, not just business."

The Concord Chamber of Commerce was founded in 1910 in response to inquiries from businesses that were considering relocating to the city. Six years later the organization achieved its first major accomplishment when it persuaded a new electric railroad line to route its tracks through the city of Concord.

After the chamber was incorporated in 1937, it became a dynamic force in Contra Costa County. In the 1940s the organization worked with the Navy to open the Naval Weapons Station in Port Chicago. During the 1950s the chamber played a prominent role in attracting new businesses, such as the Park & Shop Center, to the area.

The chamber's activity accelerated in

*One of the chamber's proudest accomplishments was bringing USAir's services to Concord.*

the 1960s and 1970s. During this time it helped create the Sister City Program with Kitakami, Japan, worked with other chambers to form the Contra Costa County Transit District, and was one of the major forces behind the construction of the Concord Pavilion.

The chamber also participated in the redevelopment of the downtown area during this period, sponsoring Concord's first Community Congress to give residents an opportunity to express their views on community development. The organization initiated the Place of Beauty program, which judges the design of new and remodeled buildings in Concord.

*The Concord Chamber of Commerce was founded in 1910 in response to inquiries from businesses that were considering relocating. Today the chamber continues in that tradition and has participated in the redevelopment of the downtown area while also retaining the city's historic nature.*

In the early 1980s the organization's Discover Concord Day was an important factor in Bank of America and Wells Fargo opening facilities in Concord, and bringing PSA/USAir to Buchanan Field. In 1984 the chamber sponsored the first Fall Fest, the popular crafts and entertainment fair that now attracts 60,000 to 80,000 people to downtown Concord every Labor Day weekend.

The chamber led the successful effort to defeat a no-growth ballot measure in 1986, making Concord unique among cities in the area.

Recently the chamber launched Leadership Concord, a 10-month educational program for Concord residents who want to get more involved in the community, and Student Leadership Day, a seminar that trains students to become future leaders in the city.

Today the chamber has more than 1,200 members—a 100-percent increase since 1981. Housed in Salvio Pacheco Square, the organization's eight full-time employees respond to requests for information from more than 200 businesses and individuals per week.

As Concord and the entire county continue to grow, the chamber will continue its role as the unified voice of the business community.

# Contra Costa Council

For more than a half-century the Contra Costa Council—a nonprofit organization of Contra Costa business leaders—has worked with local governments to stimulate business development in the county and to address the problems of growth with innovative, effective solutions.

Founded in 1936 by former State Senator Will Sharkey, the organization was originally known as the Contra Costa Development Association and was partially funded by the county. In the following decades the association helped to bring new industries to the area and to keep local business up to date on crucial bills pending in the state legislature.

In the early 1980s the 680 Corridor began to experience tremendous growth. Where thousands of Contra Costa commuters were once traveling to jobs elsewhere in the Bay Area, now some of the largest corporations were bringing employees to major complexes in Concord, Walnut Creek, and San Ramon. The need for an effective, team-oriented, private-sector organization to help tackle the accompanying new challenges was never more evident.

The council responded immediately by widening its range of services and tripling its membership. One of its most important advances was to form special task forces to recommend solutions for problems in several areas:

—The Transportation Task Force develops local sources of funding to construct needed improvements and sponsors transportation systems management programs to reduce traffic congestion through existing systems and corporate strategies—staggered shifts, carpooling, and the like.

—The Housing Task Force works to improve the supply of affordable housing near employment centers and monitors the progress of the county's General Plan Review Committee.

—The Waste Management Task Force identifies adequate landfill facilities, monitors legislation on hazardous waste management, and acts as a resource to business on waste regulations.

—The Water Task Force develops plans to ensure adequate sources of high-quality water for the county.

Today the Contra Costa Council is funded entirely by the private sector, and has 500 members representing all types of business enterprises in the county. It sponsors many noteworthy events, including Contra Costa USA, an annual conference and exposition that focuses on the business outlook for the county and presents such noted speakers as Gerald Ford, Howard K. Smith, and economist Barry Asmus. The council's monthly luncheon features local congressmen, state senators, and representatives as speakers.

The Contra Costa Update, a bimonthly newsletter published by the council, has evolved into the voice of the county's business community and is distributed to 6,000 businesses throughout Contra Costa. In 1987 the council started its own radio program on county-based KKIS to promote public discussion of topics vital to the community.

Under the leadership of current president John Carharti, the Contra Costa Council continues to support the strong partnership between the private and public sectors of the county and to maintain the quality of life that has made Contra Costa a premier area for living and doing business.

*The community of Pleasant Hill, with Mount Diablo in the background. Photo by Bob Rowan, Progressive Image*

# Armstrong Lorenz Gilmour & Whalen

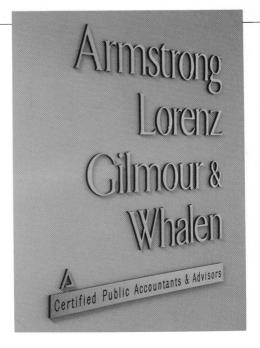

With tax law and financial markets in constant flux, the success of any organization depends to a great extent on its accounting firm, which must be able to understand the company's goals and to develop creative strategies to achieve them.

Established in 1979, the accounting firm of Armstrong Lorenz Gilmour & Whalen has provided a wide range of tax, accounting, and advisory services for numerous Northern California companies.

The firm's clients cover the breadth of Contra Costa businesses, from large real estate developers to small and mid-size retailers, construction firms, and manufacturing companies. Regardless of size, ALG&W's clients can expect a multiservice approach tailored to their immediate goals and anticipated future needs.

Just a few of ALG&W's many services

*The accounting firm of Armstrong Lorenz Gilmour & Whalen provides a variety of tax, accounting, and advisory services for a wide range of Northern California companies.*

include tax planning and forecasting, tax return preparation, audit representation, and estate planning. ALG&W also provides bookkeeping services, financial statement preparation, and in many situations functions as the client controller.

The firm's wide-ranging expertise affords clients valuable advice in many aspects of business operations. For the new business, ALG&W offers counseling on startup formation, business and financial plans, and assistance in obtaining loan financing. The established company can use ALG&W for cash-flow planning and budgeting, installing new accounting and computer systems, personnel selection and training, business acquisitions, private and public offerings, and expert testimony in litigations.

To deliver optimal service ALG&W emphasizes a high level of partner involvement—regardless of the size of the client. The partners are supported by an expert staff, recruited from the best campuses and organizations in the area. New personnel typically go through a rigorous training program that covers the latest accounting techniques and tax regulations.

ALG&W also believes that the effectiveness of the business-accountant relationship depends on constant two-way communication. To keep clients well informed, the firm conducts regular seminars on tax planning, business computer systems, employee retirement plans, and other topics vital to business success. Its quarterly newsletter contains articles on such topics as

the alternative minimum tax (AMT), passive loss allowances, cash-flow planning, life insurance, and new rules on IRAs.

Committed to the business growth of Contra Costa County, Armstrong Lorenz Gilmour & Whalen has helped many businesses in the region become more profitable. In so doing, the firm has grown as well: It employs a staff of 38 professionals headquartered in new offices at 2121 North California Boulevard in Walnut Creek.

In the years ahead Armstrong Lorenz Gilmour & Whalen will continue to provide innovative solutions to complex accounting problems, using a variety of strategies and tools. In these ever-changing, uncertain economic times, ALG&W's clients find that approach the best assurance for success.

Photo by Bob Rowan

# CHAPTER 13

Photo by Gabe Palmer/After Image

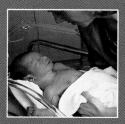

Mt. Diablo Medical Center,
162-163

John F. Kennedy University, 164

Saint Mary's College, 165

Contra Costa Community College District, 166-168

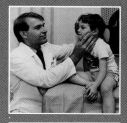

Los Medanos Community
Hospital, 169

# Quality
# of
# Life:

**M**edical and educational
institutions contribute to
the quality of life of Contra
Costa County area residents.

# Mt. Diablo Medical Center

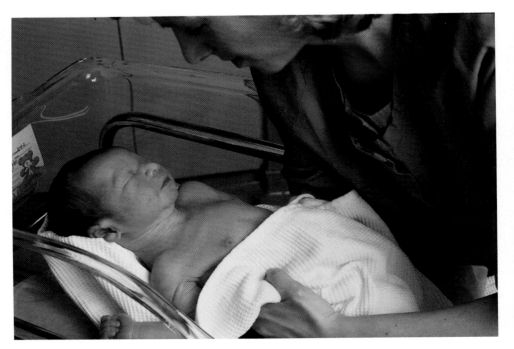

Mt. Diablo Medical Center, a nonprofit district hospital located in Concord, offers comprehensive medical care to the 700,000 residents of Contra Costa and southern Solano counties. Serving as a regional referral center for patients with heart and lung disorders, cancer, and kidney disease, the center has earned a national reputation for its innovative health care programs and development of new technology in the field of laser revascularization.

Over the years the center's medical staff has steadily grown to more than 500 physicians representing more than 30 specialties. A nursing staff of nearly 600 professionals, provides highly skilled nursing support to acute care patients and the more than 100,000 outpatients who use the hospital each year. Another 450 community volunteers play an indispensable role in helping to care for patients.

Mt. Diablo Hospital opened its doors on June 1, 1930, in a small house that served as a hospital nursing home. Founder Edna Haywood Gnotta, a Concord nurse, purchased and remodeled the facility at the request of Dr. Henry Stirwalt, who en-

*The Home Health staff trains patients to manage their care at home through skilled teaching, observation, and supervised practice.*

visioned a full-service hospital. A year later an adjacent house was converted into operating suites to expand the hospital's emergency services. Between 1958 and 1975 the hospital's three major wings were constructed, increasing capacity from 50 to the current 303 beds. Mt. Diablo has operated as a community district hospital since 1948.

Today Mt. Diablo offers more than 60 health care programs and services. The center's renowned Northern California Heart and Lung Institute provides a wide range of expertise in the prevention, diagnosis, treatment, and rehabilitation of heart and lung disease. Thirty specialists, including cardiolo-

*Mt. Diablo's Family Birthplace offers a variety of choices to meet the unique needs of each mother.*

gists, pulmonary medicine practitioners, and cardiovascular surgeons, offer their services through the institute. A Cardiac Emergency Network, linking Mt. Diablo with four other major East Bay hospitals, has recently been implemented to provide the latest acute interventional techniques for treating heart attack victims.

Dr. Garret Lee, the institute's director of clinical research, is known worldwide for his research on laser technology used to unblock clogged arteries. A modern cardiac catheterization lab with two dedicated suites for angiography is a key component of Mt. Diablo's advanced cardiac care program. In addition, more than 500 coronary bypass and valve repair surgeries are performed each year at the institute.

Mt. Diablo's Regional Cancer Center offers comprehensive diagnosis and treatment services to inpatients and outpatients. The center provides the latest screening techniques, such as low-dose mammography for early detection of breast cancer, and several educational and support groups, such as the I Can Cope program.

The hospital's expertise extends well beyond diagnosis and treatment; the medical center is equally committed to health awareness and promotion within the community. One of Mt. Diablo's wellness programs involves the former Williams Elementary School, which the hospital purchased and transformed into a modern fitness facility for the use of the public, hospital employees, and patients undergoing special-

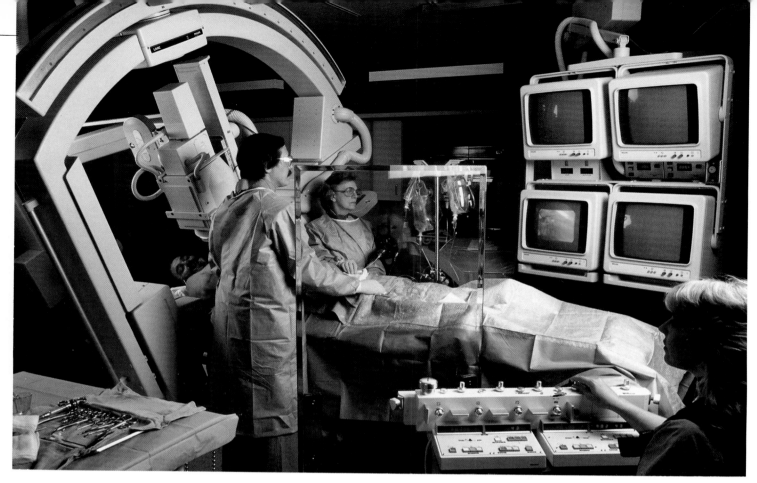

ized rehabilitation programs.

Mt. Diablo's outpatient services have increased dramatically in the past few years. The Outpatient Surgery Center helps to eliminate costly overnight hospital stays for those patients needing minor surgical procedures. The Noninvasive Cardiovascular Laboratory conducts more than 18,000 cardiovascular testing and monitoring procedures anually. The hospital's Laboratory and Diagnostic Imaging departments are open 24 hours a day, 365 days a year to provide the fastest turnaround time possible for patients. Computerized tomography (CT) scanners, magnetic resonance imaging (MRI), and conventional X-ray equipment are among the many diagnostic tools available for both inpatients and outpatients.

More than 30,000 patients utilize the hospital's Emergency Services Department each year. This fully equipped facility is prepared to meet emergency conditions, including major trauma, heart attack, stroke, and kidney failure. Trained personnel are always on duty to handle Lifeline calls from elderly and homebound patients.

To keep pace with the changing health care needs of the community, Mt. Diablo recently implemented an eating disorders program, known as Serenity. Since 1980 the medical center has offered an inpatient chemical dependency program that has achieved an excellent record in treating substance abuse. The newly remodeled Family Birthplace offers personalized maternity care and a comfortable setting. Four labor and de-

*Above: Mt. Diablo Medical Center performs more than 1,200 cardiac catheterizations annually in the new and expanded cardiac catheterization laboratory.*

*Right: Once diagnosis is made, the Regional Cancer Center staff provides state-of-the-art treatment, while minimizing patients' discomfort. Patients with cancer receive comprehensive care in either the inpatient Cancer Unit or as outpatients.*

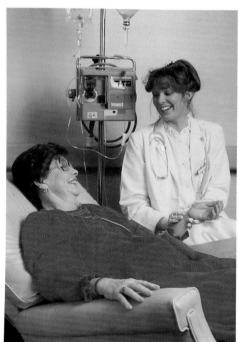

livery rooms and an Alternative Birthing Center serve the needs of expectant mothers and their families.

Today's health care environment places an increasing emphasis on the convenient delivery of health care. In response, Mt. Diablo has developed several programs to extend hospital services off-site from the main hospital complex. The Home Health Care Program, for example, provides a variety of nursing services and training to homebound patients. Mt. Diablo's Senior Care program simplifies access to senior services.

Mt. Diablo's reputation for innovative programs and quality health care has attracted some of the top physicians in the country to Concord. Modern offices, such as the award-winning Mt. Diablo Medical Office Building, developed as a joint venture between the hospital and a group of staff physicians, reflect the harmonious relations that exist between the two groups.

Community support has always been a major asset to the hospital. Over the years

many dedicated community volunteers have donated their time and talents to the hospital. In 1987 the community donated more than $500,000 to the foundation.

The widespread reputation of Mt. Diablo for excellence in patient care may be attributed to the dedication of the people involved with the medical center. Working together, the board of directors, administration, medical staff, and 1,400 dedicated health care professionals keep Mt. Diablo Medical Center on the leading edge of emerging health care programs and services.

# John F. Kennedy University

On October 4, 1965, 60 students attended the first classes of John F. Kennedy University held in Charter Hall, a former mortuary in Martinez. Today the university enrolls 2,000 students and holds classes at a main campus in Orinda and at nine other centers in five Bay Area counties.

Behind this remarkable and rapid success was the vision of founding president Harry L. Morrison; his wife, Georgia; and Lind M. Higgins. Morrison, founder of the public administration program at St. Mary's College in 1961, conceived the university as the first university in the nation dedicated solely to adult learning. Since prospective students would have job and family responsibilities and would not be able to attend full time or during the day, classes were offered on evenings and weekends.

The faculty would include not only top-flight scholars from academia, but also leaders in business and government. This focus on faculty composed of experienced professionals has set John F. Kennedy University apart from other universities and is still the foundation of the school's motto: "We practice what we teach."

During its early years the university struggled financially, depending on individuals and institutions who donated money, services, furniture, or equipment. Instructors agreed to defer salaries, and staff contrib-

uted services that were later estimated at $175,000. Classes met in alcoves of the former mortuary, the president's office, or other impromptu settings.

By 1974, however, the university had found its niche and was on firm financial ground. Serving the needs of 440 students, the school had outgrown the confines of Charter Hall, and classes were held in rooms rented from public schools in Martinez and Orinda, and in private offices in Walnut Creek, Berkeley, and other nearby communities.

These scattered classrooms also proved inadequate. In the fall of 1975 grants from several major foundations enabled the university to relocate to its present main campus in Orinda.

John F. Kennedy University attained its most significant goal in 1977, when it was accredited by the Western Association of Schools and Colleges. By this time Robert M. Fisher, a scholar, civic leader, lawyer, and entrepreneur, had taken over the reins of the university from Morrison, who died in 1974. Dr. Fisher is generally given credit for raising the funds necessary for the relocation and for establishing several full-salaried core faculty positions.

The university's second decade saw considerable growth in number of students, facil-

*John F. Kennedy University first held classes in 1965 in a former mortuary in Martinez. Today, with an enrollment of 2,000 students, it is accredited by the Western Association of Schools and Colleges and is a pioneer in adult learning.*

ities, and degree programs. By 1984, 1,900 students were enrolled, and the school was operating within a $6-million annual budget. A new computer system, installed in 1982, helped meet the challenge of the school's rapidly increasing enrollment.

Today John F. Kennedy University offers a juris doctor degree in law and bachelor's and master's degree programs in such diverse fields as liberal studies, business administration, management, clinical psychology, holistic health education, interior design, museum studies, textiles, and transpersonal and holistic counseling.

The university employs an administrative staff of 180 and an adjunct faculty of more than 500 leaders in their chosen fields. Its instructors are professionals who share with students at night what they do for a living during the day.

The school's 2,000 students come from all parts of the United States and 25 foreign countries; with an average age of 36, they have unusually diverse professional and personal backgrounds. Small, personalized classes—offered year round with a convenient evening and weekend schedule—encourage full student participation.

As the pioneer in adult learning, John F. Kennedy University knew long ago what many other institutions of higher learning are discovering now—that lifelong learning benefits not only the individual but the entire community. Today John F. Kennedy University continues to practice what it teaches and to expand its influence throughout the nation and the world.

# Saint Mary's College

Nestled in the rolling hills of Moraga, Saint Mary's College of California offers a comprehensive array of undergraduate, graduate, and extended education programs. Known for its academic excellence and personalized instruction, the college boasts a long tradition of dedication to classical Christian principles of education.

Saint Mary's moved to its present 420-acre site in the Moraga Valley of Contra Costa in 1928.

The Moraga years have been marked by expansion of academic programs and the school's physical plant. Since 1969, under current president Brother Mel Anderson, FSC, the college has added graduate and extended education, and built such facilities as McKeon Pavilion, LeFevre Theatre, the Soda Activity Center, and several student residence halls. It has also increased enrollment and added financial aid programs.

Today Saint Mary's is a coeducational institution with a student body of 2,400 undergraduates and a total enrollment of 3,400. Its academic program is organized into five schools: liberal arts, science, economics and business administration, education, and extended education. The college co-sponsors an intercollegiate nursing program with Samuel E. Merritt Hospital in Oakland.

Graduate programs are offered in business, international business, psychology, health, physical education and recreation, and education. The curricula of extended ed-

*The Saint Mary's campus, distinguished by the College Chapel, is a truly serene and beautiful setting.*

ucation includes paralegal, management, health services administration, and continuing education programs.

Saint Mary's alumni hold leadership positions in business and industry both in Contra Costa and nationwide. Among Saint Mary's noted county alumni are Ken Hofmann, builder and developer; George Gordon, a founder of Contra Costa's community college system; and Tom Candiotti, pitcher for the Cleveland Indians. The devotion of SMC alumni is well known—the college ranks in the top 5 percent of U.S. colleges in the percentage of alumni who contribute to their alma mater.

While Contra Costa offers a wide

range of services to Saint Mary's, the college offers a great deal to the county. The school's meeting and conference facilities are regularly used for civic and community functions.

The Saint Mary's Executives' Symposium, founded in 1957, attracts major business leaders from Contra Costa and across the country. In addition, all Saint Mary's athletic and cultural events, the Hearst Art Gallery, and the Saint Albert Library are open to the public.

One of the oldest colleges in the West, Saint Mary's was founded in 1863 in San Francisco by Archbishop Joseph Alemany. The Christian Brothers, the largest Catholic order devoted exclusively to teaching, assumed directorship of the college in 1868—a major factor in the college's reputation and success over the past 120 years.

In 1889 Saint Mary's moved to Oakland, where the school survived two devastating fires, the 1906 earthquake, and several financial crises. Through it all, the college emerged stronger, more formalized, and more diversified, as art, engineering, and law were added to the curricula and the school's athletic teams gained national prominence.

During its 125-year history, Saint Mary's College has remained firmly committed to academic achievement. With the ongoing support of alumni and the community, Saint Mary's will continue to use the lessons of the past to carve new legacies of excellence in the future.

*The Christian Brothers provide Saint Mary's with direction and an academic philosophy derived from their founder, St. John Baptiste De La Salle. In this picture Brother Kenneth Cardwell, FSC, leads a seminar class.*

# Contra Costa Community College District

When Contra Costa citizens approved a referendum establishing the Contra Costa Community College District, only the concept existed for a countywide system of two-year colleges. The year was 1948 and most of the county was rural, just awakening to postwar suburbanization and business growth.

Forty years later the district serves the county's varied educational and vocational needs with three respected institutions—Contra Costa College in San Pablo, Diablo Valley College in Pleasant Hill, and Los Medanos College in Pittsburg. Together these three schools enroll more than 35,000

students, many of whom transfer to four-year institutions in California and across the nation.

With boundaries roughly the same as Contra Costa County, the district covers 686 square miles, making it one of the largest college districts in California. The district's central offices are located in Martinez, and the district is directed by a five-member governing board, headed by chancellor Jack Carhart.

The district's colleges are distinguished by their academic excellence, their focus on vocational programs, and their wide range of student services—career counseling, child-care facilities, services for the disabled, and financial aid programs. The school's low tuition (five dollars per credit and never more than $50) ensures participa-

tion of all social and economic groups.

### Contra Costa College

As the first college of the new district, Contra Costa College opened its doors in February 1950 as West Contra Costa Junior College. Only 500 students were on hand for classes held in a group of vacant World War II shipyard buildings at Point Richmond. Today Contra Costa College spreads across an 83-acre site in San Pablo and enrolls more than 7,500 students.

The college offers more than 800 courses each semester, including those that lead to an Associate of Arts or Associate of Science degree or a Certificate of Achievement. The curricula include architectural drafting, business, computer informa-

tion systems, electronics, engineering, interior design, management, and a wide array of liberal arts courses.

The school's vocational programs enjoy a solid reputation in several occupational areas, including automobile mechanics, medical and dental assisting, early childhood education, registered nursing, and real estate brokering.

Recognizing the rich cultural heritage of the west county population it serves, the school also offers programs in Asian, Afro-American, Hispanic, Native American, and Women's Studies.

The campus of Contra Costa College includes several modern facilities designed to complement classroom learning. The library has more than 53,000 volumes, a broad selection of journals and newspapers, and an extensive reference collection. A Media Center houses a wide variety of records, films, and video and audio tapes. The school's Computer Laboratories contain numerous PCs and are open for general student use.

Over the years Contra Costa has established a strong bond with the community. Residents of the west county regularly attend art exhibits, music recitals, theatrical productions, athletic events, and special lectures and presentations held at the school. Members of the community enjoy use of the library, Performing Arts Center, and physical fitness facilities.

The county's business and community

leaders also play an active and vital role in the college. Advisory committees, composed of local business leaders, ensure that the curricula in occupational fields reflect the up-to-date practices of business and industry and are meeting community needs. The Contra Costa College Foundation—a nonprofit corporation composed of leaders from business, industry, and education—raises funds to support scholarships and awards, improvement of instructional facilities, purchase of equipment, cultural programs and events, and staff development.

### Diablo Valley College

When Diablo Valley College (DVC) began operations in 1951, many of the communities surrounding the Pleasant Hill Campus were rural. Today it serves a population of some 300,000 people living in the vigorous urban/suburban environment of central Contra Costa County.

DVC's respected position in the academic community has evolved over four decades. Over the years DVC has transferred more students each year to four-year colleges and to the University of California, Berkeley, than any community college in the state.

The college is also noted for its fine vocational curriculum. It offers more than 30 oc-

cupational programs that draw students from all over the Bay Area. DVC's Hotel and Restaurant Management program, for example, has trained hundreds of students for management careers in the U.S. hospitality industry. The school's programs in dental hygiene, electronics, library and media services, and early childhood education are fulfilling a growing need for trained people in these professions.

The school makes a special effort to bring education to the community. A new satellite campus, the Center for Higher Education in the Bishop Ranch Business Park in San Ramon, offers classes at convenient times for employees of businesses in the development. Early-morning and drive-time classes have been extremely successful, and the center's enrollment reached 3,000 for the spring 1988 semester. Students enrolled at the Center for Higher Education— a shared venture with U.C. Berkeley Extension and Cal State Hayward—can take courses from any of the three institutions.

The Diablo Valley campus boasts a new state-of-the-art computer lab, a performing arts complex that is a mainstay of the area's cultural life, and fine athletic facilities used extensively by the community.

### Los Medanos College

The district's third college, Los Meda-

nos (LMC), began operations in 1974 to serve the entire eastern portion of Contra Costa County. Located on a 120-acre site near the boundary between Pittsburg and Antioch, Los Medanos enrolls approximately 6,000 students.

LMC offers more than 300 academic and vocational courses and many specialized programs in such areas as appliance service, cosmetology, emergency medical technology, registered nursing, fire technology, recording arts, recreation education, and welding technology. The school's cooperative work program gives students on-the-job experience at businesses throughout the county.

The school's additional evening and Saturday classes attract many people with regular jobs and responsibilities that prevent their attending college during weekday hours. Opportunities are available for those

with the Contra Costa business community and local governments. Instructors meet regularly with business, labor, and industrial representatives to discuss curriculum and job market demands. Recently LMC started a program to provide training for new businesses and leaders for the city of Pittsburg's "incentive zone," a reduced-tax zone that encourages building and business development. Many local businesses and firms use the college's ample facilities for meetings. Many instructors are employed in local businesses, which helps keep Los Medanos up on the latest innovations in business and industry.

The college's good working relationship with community youth projects is well-known throughout the community. The institution annually co-sponsors the Summer Youth Jobs Program, and in spring 1988 the college started the Two-Plus-Two program, which integrates high school vocational classes with LMC classes and prepares students to continue vocational education, learn high-tech trades, and develop good work habits.

who wish to learn or improve a vocational skill, who are working toward a college degree, or who merely want to broaden their general education.

Cited in the *Chronicle of Higher Education* and the *Wall Street Journal* as a leader in community college education, the school awards Associate in Arts and Associate in Science degrees and Certificates of Achievement in a wide variety of academic and vocational programs. Approximately 40 courses are offered in business, ranging from accounting to typing to medical transcription. The LMC Business Lab offers students the opportunity to apply the knowledge gained in classroom settings.

LMC's recording arts program, featuring state-of-the-art facilities and experienced instructors, covers studio procedures, record producing, video film production, and other aspects of the recording/video business.

LMC maintains a close relationship

# Los Medanos Community Hospital

For more than four decades Los Medanos Community Hospital (LMCH) has provided comprehensive health care to East Contra Costa County. Located on the Pittsburg-Antioch border, LMCH is a fully accredited, 81-bed, acute care facility that offers a top-notch medical staff, a wide range of medical specialties, community health care services, and the most up-to-date medical technology.

Originally known as Pittsburg Community Hospital, Los Medanos first opened its doors in 1945. Built by the federal government to serve Camp Stoneman and other war-related industries in the Pittsburg area, the hospital was the most modern of its time in the Bay Area. After the war the newly formed Pittsburg Community Hospital District purchased the medical institution for use by the entire community.

During the 1950s and 1960s the hospital grew in size and services. Many physicians were attracted by the growing industrial and residential community, the available technology, and the excellent reputation of the nursing staff.

*The main entrance of Los Medanos Community Hospital.*

In 1972, when the need for expansion became apparent, the hospital board approved the purchase of 20 acres of land at LMCH's present location at Loveridge and Leland roads. In 1976, supported by community tax and bond measures, ground was broken for a new hospital, which was completed on July 12, 1979.

Today Los Medanos is the largest and best-equipped hospital in East Contra Costa, with 175 staff physicians representing 40 medical specialties. Its highly trained nurses, therapists, and technicians give patients competent, compassionate care.

Over the past few years Los Medanos has added modern equipment that enables the hospital's staff to take advantage of the newest medical procedures. The radiology department has acquired a new 24-hour CT scanner, digital subtraction angiography, ultrasound, low-dose mammography, and nuclear medicine technology. The surgery department has implemented fluoroscopy and state-of-the-art equipment for performing knee and shoulder arthroscopies, and prostate and bladder surgery. New cardiology equipment includes pulmonary and cardiac stress testing, echocardiology, 24-hour portable heart monitoring, and automated blood pressure monitoring.

Along with the technological advances, many new community service programs have been introduced at the hospital. The Living Alone program helps surviving family members cope with the death of a loved one. The I Can Cope and Take Control programs help cancer and diabetes victims lead productive lives. A pregnancy and parenting education program offers classes on pregnancy exercises, mother-baby exercises, postpartum support, and parenthood. A wide range of benefits for senior citizens, including health maintenance tips and meal discounts in the hospital's dining room, are part of the 65 Plus and Silver Dining Club programs. Finally, LMCH has programs for weight control, smoking cessation, and mid-life crises.

The support of East Contra Costa County residents has enabled LMCH to grow and change to meet the needs of the community. With the county's continued support and involvement, Los Medanos Community Hospital will provide health care for years to come.

*Dr. Timothy Greco examines a pediatric patient in the Emergency Room.*

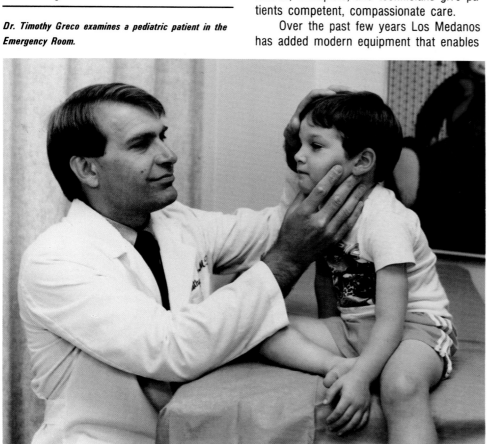

# CHAPTER 14

Wentling Photography,
172-173

Photo by Gabe Palmer/After Image

Sunvalley Shopping Center, 174-175

Longs Drugstores, 176-177

CONCO Cement Company, 178-179

Lafayette Park Hotel, 180-181

Concord Hilton, 182-183

# THE
# MARKETPLACE:

The area's retail establishments, service industries, and products are enjoyed by residents and visitors to the area.

# Wentling Photography

When Contra Costa businesses and individuals need photographic services, they have to look no further than their own backyard: Wentling Photography, with eight locations in the county, has been the area's premier photography center for more than 40 years.

Wentling offers professional portrait photography, on-location photography, on-site lab processing, camera equipment, and custom framing and matting services. Led by the Wentling family, now in its third generation, all Wentling locations provide professionally trained photographers and sales staff, who guide customers and clients to the right choices.

"We're certainly not your run-of-the-mill camera store," says Thomas Wentling, president of the company. "We offer expertise and years of experience—whether we're taking the photos or the customer is. Our long-term commitment to Contra Costa also distinguishes us from the rest of the pack. We're very sensitive to serving the needs of the community. After all, we've been here for more than 40 years."

The venture was founded in 1945, when Marie Wentling began to turn her photography hobby into a thriving business in the family's Concord garage. While Marie

took portraits, her husband, Harry, picked up rolls of film left by customers at several retail stores in the area and processed them in the Wentling "studio." By the early 1950s business had become so good the couple was forced to move to a more spacious studio, located at Mt. Diablo and Concord Avenue in downtown Concord.

*Wentling Photography is still run by the Wentling family. Pictured here are (in the background, from left) some of the third generation—Scott Wentling, Ben Wentling, Dirk Wentling, and Patti Baggett. In the foreground is Tom Wentling, a second-generation family member.*

*Harry Wentling, co-founder of Wentling's, in front of the first Wentling's sign, circa 1945.*

From these proverbial mom-and-pop origins, the company has grown to more than 65 people employed in eight Contra Costa locations: Concord, Walnut Creek, Antioch, Danville, Lafayette, Moraga, San Ramon, and the Sunvalley Mall. Always a family-owned and -operated business, the firm is presently headed by Thomas Wentling, Marie and Harry's son. His three sons and one daughter also play key roles in the organization: Dirk manages Wentling's portrait studio; Ben is the general manager of the retail camera store operations; Scott runs the company's processing labs; and Patricia directs the company's marketing department.

"Over the years," says Thomas Wentling, "the key to our success has been diversification. As the needs of the community have changed, our products and services have changed to accommodate those needs."

In the early 1980s Wentling was a pioneer in rapid-turnover lab processing,

*Here Dirk Wentling stands with some old and new equipment used in the studio.*

ties—differ significantly from business portraits in terms of preparation and communication between photographer and subject.

"And even within the field of business photography, there are significant differences," Dirk explains. "The photographer must know the differences in audience and setting. The portrait hanging on the executive's wall must convey something different than the one published in an annual report or a promotional brochure."

Meeting the needs of a wide range of clientele requires years of on-the-job experience, continuing education, and recertification by professional societies. Dirk is certified by the Professional Photographers of America, Tom and Ben by the Photography Marketing Association (Tom is also the vice-president of the international association), and Scott by the Society of Photo Finishing Engineers.

The Wentling dedication to excellence has reaped the company several honors, including the Photographic Retailer of the Year Award from the National Brand Names Foundation in 1966.

Wentling Photography has grown with the community by actively participating in its civic affairs. Thomas Wentling is a former city council member of Concord, the city's current treasurer, and a former president of the Concord Chamber of Commerce. Dirk is a former vice-president of the Concord chamber.

Though Wentling Photography continues to expand to meet the needs of Contra Costa County, the company still retains many aspects of a family business. "Many of our customers rely on us as a source of experience," notes Dirk Wentling, "just as they rely on their own families."

*State-of-the-art processing equipment is used at the many Wentling one-hour labs countywide.*

soon to become a major trend in film developing. Unlike many one-hour film processors, however, all Wentling lab work is done in house, resulting in enhanced quality control and customer satisfaction. The company's film-processing laboratories are some of the most sophisticated in the East Bay, boasting state-of-the-art equipment that can "cover" a customer's mistake or achieve a special effect with equal ease.

In the 1980s, as Contra Costa evolved from a residential suburb into a bustling business and industrial center, Wentling entered the field of business photography. "We've done all types of business photography—for small and large businesses alike," says Dirk Wentling. "From highly stylized portraiture for the walls of executive suites to full-color and black-and-white photos used in corporate publications and brochures to very detailed shots for corporate litigation."

Portrait photography is a subtle art form, of course, requiring taste, technical skill, and the ability to work with people. Over the years the studio has developed a classical style of portraiture that a knowing observer can recognize immediately as a Wentling portrait. Portrait work is also highly specialized: Wedding and children's portraits—both longtime Wentling special-

# Sunvalley Shopping Center

The old adage, "Change is a constant," can certainly be applied to Contra Costa. It also applies to Sunvalley Mall—the largest, most successful shopping center in Northern California. Over the years Sunvalley has kept pace with change by keeping in touch with shoppers. New shops and services have been added, stores have been remodeled and modernized, and new events have been held—all in response to the changing tastes and needs of shoppers.

Located on a 79-acre site at Willow Pass Road and Interstate 680, Sunvalley's 1.4 million square feet of shopping space houses 160 stores, restaurants, theaters, and services that together employ 5,000 people and serve millions of customers each year. It is no surprise that Sunvalley is Concord's largest retail tax contributor.

A wide selection of stores and merchandise has always been Sunvalley's strong suit. While most shopping centers offer two major department stores, Sunvalley boasts four. The range of merchandise offered at these and other stores at the two-tiered center is among the most comprehensive in the country.

The Sunvalley ground breaking took place in the summer of 1965, and two years later, on August 5, 1967, the center cele-

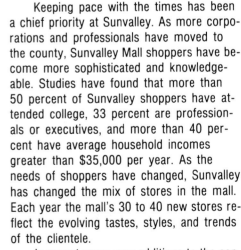

*Macy's is one of four department store anchors for Sunvalley Shopping Center.*

brated its grand opening. At the time Sunvalley was not only the largest retail center in the region but also the largest enclosed, environmentally controlled retail center in the world.

The center opened with three of its four department stores—JCPenney, Macy's, and Sears. The fourth department store, Emporium-Capwell, joined the center in 1981. Over the years all have undergone extensive multimillion-dollar renovations to keep up with the latest style and service enhancements and customer needs.

Keeping pace with the times has been a chief priority at Sunvalley. As more corporations and professionals have moved to the county, Sunvalley Mall shoppers have become more sophisticated and knowledgeable. Studies have found that more than 50 percent of Sunvalley shoppers have attended college, 33 percent are professionals or executives, and more than 40 percent have average household incomes greater than $35,000 per year. As the needs of shoppers have changed, Sunvalley has changed the mix of stores in the mall. Each year the mall's 30 to 40 new stores reflect the evolving tastes, styles, and trends of the clientele.

In recent years new additions to the center include an expanded Limited store that will serve as a prototype; Eddie Bauer and American Eagle Outfitters, two outdoorwear stores that cater to the growing interest in casual clothing; Career Image and Caren Charles, which offer stylish business apparel for professional women; The Bombay Company, which features reproductions of English furnishings; and Electronics Boutique and Home Computing Center, stores

*The Bombay Company, which features reproductions of antique English furnishings, is just one of Sunvalley's new stores.*

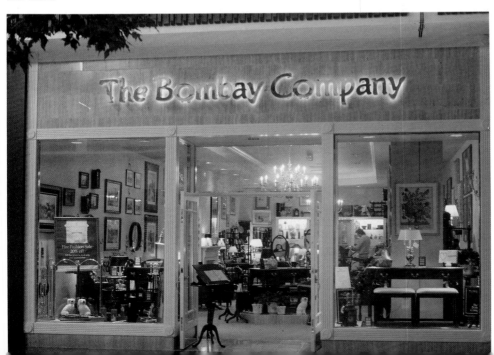

*Located on a 79-acre site at Willow Pass Road and Interstate 680, Sunvalley's 1.4 million square feet of shopping includes 160 stores.*

that serve the growing interest in electronics.

When the mall's regular roster of shops is considered, Sunvalley offers an array of retail choices. The center has beauty salons, bookstores, stationery shops, luggage stores, and toy stores, as well as stores specializing in sporting goods, eyeglasses, hobbies, and greeting cards. Restaurants feature fine Italian, Chinese, and French cuisine. In home furnishings, Sunvalley's specialty stores carry a complete range of merchandise for every room in the house.

More than three dozen shops offer a wide selection of contemporary women's fashions—from the latest European styles to fashions with a California flair. For men, Sunvalley offers a wide choice of handsome clothing—suits of all cuts and styles, outdoor gear, beachwear, and shoes for home or the office.

The customer service center is a focal point at Sunvalley. Located in the middle of the mall, the center is staffed with experienced personnel ready to assist customers in finding specific stores and merchandise. Gift certificates, strollers, and wheelchairs are available at the center as standard conveniences. As a special service for both merchants and patrons, the customer service center also provides listings of employment opportunities within the mall.

Given its wide range of merchandise

and services, it is not surprising that Sunvalley serves a wide trade area that virtually blankets the East Bay. Serving three counties—Contra Costa, Alameda, and Solano—Sunvalley draws shoppers from as far north as Vallejo, as far south as San Ramon, as far east as Antioch, and as far west as El Sobrante. To accommodate the steady flow of shoppers, the center provides parking for more than 7,400 cars.

As a dynamic part of the community, Sunvalley actively participates in many health and charitable functions. The mall holds blood drives four times per year in its special community room. In conjunction with the local chapter of the American Heart Association and Mt. Diablo Medical Center, Sunvalley sponsors its popular Mall Walking program in which the shopping center is turned into a course for exercise-conscious citizens between 7 a.m. and 10 a.m.: Walkers receive maps of the mall, suggested routes, materials on the health benefits of walking, and "I'Mall For It" T-shirts when they complete 100 miles.

Looking ahead to the future, Sunvalley's management sees continued growth for the region—which means continuing changes for the mall. Among other things, the center is planning an extensive remodeling to keep up with shoppers' needs and conveniences. Though this kind of project might be difficult for some organizations, it shouldn't be difficult for the Sunvalley Mall—an institution that has so much experience with change.

*The two-level shopping center features the widest selection of stores in all of Contra Costa County, in addition to restaurants and services.*

# Longs Drugstores

Beginning with just one store and some unique retailing ideas, Longs Drugs has evolved into one of the largest and most successful drugstore chains in the nation. Today the company operates more than 235 "super" drugstores across the country and posts annual sales of nearly $2 billion.

Founded by two brothers, Joe and Tom Long, the first Longs drugstore opened on Piedmont Avenue in Oakland in May 1938. In one of the earliest and most innovative uses of direct mail, the brothers sent personal letters to thousands of potential customers, announcing the opening.

*Above right: In May 1938 Joe and Tom Long opened their first drugstore on Piedmont Avenue in Oakland. With a good selection of over-the-counter and prescription medicines, Longs offered a wide variety of personal and household products, and introduced a policy of "service in a self-service store."*

*Below: Brothers Joe (right) and Tom Long (far left), founders of Longs Drugstores, and Bob Long (center), son of Joe, president of one of the most successful drugstore chains in the nation.*

Taped to each letter was a shiny new penny—the reward for shopping at Longs.

The creative use of direct mail was merely a prelude to several innovations in the store itself. In addition to a good selection of over-the-counter remedies and prescription medicines, Longs offered a wide array of other personal and household products. According to one newspaper account the new operation had "the largest and most complete selection in the Bay Region."

In addition, the store introduced a self-service policy, one of the first in the retail drug industry. Finally, the store offered all its products at extremely low prices.

Though the store had its supporters, many critics predicted that the venture would fail: "Nobody can sell that cheap and stay in business" was the oft-heard refrain.

Obviously, the business did not fail. Just 10 months later the Long brothers opened their second store in what would eventually become a 235-store network over the next half-century. Today Bob Long, son of co-founder Joe Long, serves as president of the thriving drug chain.

Longs entered Contra Costa County in 1958, when the El Cerrito store opened. The 14th store in the chain, the El Cerrito store was the largest of its kind and employed 40 people, an unheard-of number in that era.

Throughout the next two decades Longs stores began opening almost everywhere in the county—in San Pablo, Concord, Pinole, Walnut Creek, Antioch, Clayton, Moraga, and Pittsburg. Burgeoning growth along the Highway 24-680 corridor prompted further additions to the Longs chain in Danville, Pleasant Hill, San Ramon, and Martinez.

Today Longs operates 14 stores in Contra Costa. In 1970 the company moved its headquarters from Oakland to Walnut Creek, where it has expanded twice to accommodate additional accounting, legal, training, and merchandising personnel.

Store autonomy sets Longs apart from other retail drugstore chains. Each store operates as a separate entity, attuned to the

vice organizations. For example, Bill Combs, treasurer and vice-president/ administration, served as mayor of Moraga, is chairman of the board of John Muir Medical Center, and is president of the California Taxpayers' Association.

This kind of active participation is indicative of Longs' civic-mindedness—community service goes back a long way in the company's history. Joe and Tom Long provided major funding for the School of Pharmacy at the University of the Pacific. Joe contributed considerable resources for a new addition to the University of California Medical Center, and Tom and his wife, Billy, have been actively involved in the John Muir Medical Center in Walnut Creek since its inception. Tom Long was named Citizen of the Year by the Walnut Creek Chamber of Commerce for his service to the community.

Longs stores sponsor community baseball teams, support high school yearbooks and publications, and participate in service clubs throughout Contra Costa County. At Christmas time, employees of Longs general offices and its fixture shop build handmade toys for the Toys for Tots campaign.

Whether for the community or the customer, Longs has built its success on a 50-year tradition of service and caring.

needs of the community in which it is located. Independent Longs managers function as local entrepreneurs, responsible for buying, merchandising, and staffing their own stores. Because Longs stores are customized to the cities and counties they serve, they become an integral part of these communities.

All Longs stores, however, contain threads of continuity. Because Longs views its pharmacies as community health centers, each store is first and foremost a drugstore. All stores have cosmetics and photo departments, and all service departments are staffed by specially trained personnel. "Service in a self-service store" is a longtime tradition at Longs.

As a corporation, Longs is also unique in its self-sufficiency. The company builds its own store fixtures, produces its own video programs in a Longs-owned and -operated studio, and designs its own retail management software.

Over the years the firm has been delighted with Contra Costa County, both as a location for many of its stores and as a base for its general offices. Longs has taken advantage of the county's highly skilled labor pool to staff its headquarters. Most of Longs key executives live in the county, and many are active in civic and ser-

*Customized to the cities and counties they serve, Longs stores have become an integral part of these communities. In addition, all departments are staffed by specially trained personnel.*

*Today Longs operates more than 235 "super" drugstores and posts annual sales of nearly $2 billion.*

# CONCO Cement Company

When cement mason Matt Gonsalves founded CONCO Cement Company in 1959, he never dreamed his new venture would someday be the second-largest concrete contractor in the nation. One clue to CONCO's growth is its weekly payroll: The firm's first weekly payroll in 1959 was $800. Today that same payroll averages $300,000.

The venture started out as a five-way partnership with Matt's brothers, William and John, and Gerald and Raymond Santucci, all of whom were in the construction trades. With Matt's home in Concord serving as CONCO's first offices, the company focused primarily on small residential projects—patios, driveways, and the like.

It wasn't long, however, before Contra Costa home owners learned of the firm's reliability and craftsmanship: By the end of the first year CONCO was forced to increase its payroll to 20 employees. By 1972 CONCO had outgrown Gonsalves' home office, forcing the company to move

to a small shop on Monument Boulevard in Concord. Four years later this facility also proved to be inadequate, and the firm relocated to its present headquarters at 5151 Port Chicago Highway.

However, the real growth for the company began in the mid-1970s, when CONCO entered the commercial and industrial construction market. Since that time the organization has been the prime concrete contractor on some of the largest office buildings, hotels, medical facilities, shopping centers, and parking garages in the Bay Area.

Just a small sampling of projects gives a good idea of the firm's wide range of construction skills: Office buildings—The Bayside Plaza and the Bakewell Brown buildings in San Francisco, and the Bank of America office and parking complex in Concord; Hotels—Marriott Hotel in San Francisco, Hyatt Regency Hotel in Burlingame, and the Techmart and Doubletree Hotel in Santa Clara; Retail centers—Hilltop Mall and the Sunvalley Shopping Center in Contra Costa; Medical facilities—Veterans' Hospital, John Muir Hospital, and Concord Hospital, all in Contra Costa County; and Marine docks—Rincon Point Marina, just

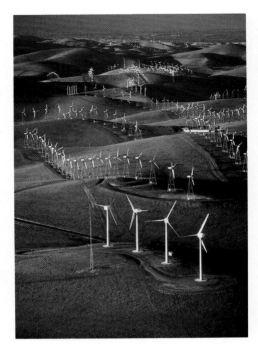

*Windpower structures, installed by CONCO for the U.S. Windpower Agency, line the rolling hills of Altamont Pass. Photo by Steve Proehl*

*One of CONCO's major commercial projects was the Bank of America office and parking complex in downtown Concord, built in 1985. Photo by Steve Proehl*

*This precast floating dock system in San Francisco Bay was manufactured at CONCO's Pleasanton facility. Photo by Steve Proehl*

*Right: The Villages, in San Jose, is one of many CONCO residential projects. Photo by Steve Proehl*

south of the Oakland Bay Bridge in San Francisco.

In addition, CONCO is still involved in residential projects, such as the Bayview housing development in Richmond, The Villages in San Jose, and California Harbor in Oakley. Many of the firm's residential projects were built with special CONCO-patented precast foundation systems that are manufactured in the company's Pleasanton facility and are state of the art in minimizing house movement.

Today CONCO Cement Company has more than 400 employees and some of the most advanced concrete-placing equipment in the industry, including a fleet of 30 concrete pumps that can handle the most complex skyscraper or hillside project. In 1987 CONCO placed more than 400,000 cubic yards of concrete for its numerous commercial and residential buildings—enough concrete to fill a four-foot-wide sidewalk stretching from San Francisco to Chicago.

In accord with its long tradition of service, the corporation handles projects of all sizes for all budgets—from a young family's first home to million-dollar homes in modern residential developments, from small suburban office centers to massive office buildings, and from floating concrete docks to complex specialty projects.

One such specialty project was the Teleport Towers, which the firm constructed on a steep hill in Sunol using helicopters. Another was the picturesque windmills in

Altamont Pass that generate much of the wind power for East Bay utilities.

With a large, experienced staff of estimators and project managers, the company can prepare preliminary budgets and develop cost-analysis and value-engineering reports.

The organization continues to be owned and managed by the Gonsalves and Santucci families. Matt's son, Steven Gonsalves, who was practically raised in the concrete construction industry, is now president and chief operating officer.

Boasting nearly 30 years in the county and a longtime reputation for service and integrity, CONCO Cement Company provides a solid foundation for Contra Costa business progress.

# Lafayette Park
# Hotel

In a nation overflowing with massive concrete-and-glass hotels, it is refreshing to find a hotel with the grace of the traditional European château. With its Norman French architectural style, gracious service, and modern amenities, the new Lafayette Park Hotel manages to combine the charm of a European resort with the conveniences of the best American business hotels.

Stepping into the lobby of the Lafayette Park is like stepping into another, more elegant era. Hand-carved curving oak staircases ascend three stories into a 50-foot open-air turret. A cozy private library contains a wood-burning fireplace that is covered by a seventeenth-century white-marble mantlepiece imported from Provence, France.

As in the classical inns of Europe, the rooms surround separate courtyards. One courtyard boasts a hand-carved Italian limestone obelisk fountain. A classic stone wishing well sits demurely in another.

The spacious, soundproof guest rooms feature king- and double-queen-size beds

*Right: The Lafayette Park Hotel combines the amenities of an American business hotel with the charm and tradition of a European resort.*

*Below: The lobby contains a hand-carved oak staircase.*

with carved cherrywood headboards and side tables, armoires that conceal color television sets, and comfortable sitting areas with large desks. Gracing the walls are print reproductions of French hunting scenes, balloon rides, and floral still-life paintings. Each room has a wet bar and refrigerator, and many have fireplaces, balconies, dormer windows, and vaulted ceilings. Even the bathrooms glow with special cinnamon cloud granite quarried in India.

Built in 1986, the Lafayette Park was a community project from the start. The citizens of Lafayette desired a grand hotel that would fit the character of the city and its terrain. Designed by the firm of Crosby, Thornton, and Marshall, the hotel blends nat-

*The Duck Club Restaurant, located within the hotel, specializes in imaginative regional American cuisine. Pictured here is the entrance to the restaurant.*

urally into a surrounding hillside, giving it the feel of a charming country inn.

Since its opening the Lafayette Park has been the setting of many conferences and receptions sponsored by local businesses, civic organizations, and community service groups. The Lafayette Citizen of the Year dinner, for example, is held annually at the hotel, as well as the Lafayette Concours de Elegance Preview Party and the Chamber of Commerce Bridal Faire and Business Trade Show. The establishment has also become a standard retreat for entertainers performing at the Concord Pavilion and Rheem Theatre, as well as a hideaway for business VIPs looking for a respite from hectic social schedules.

The hotel provides facilities and numerous amenities for both the business and vacation traveler. Three spacious conference-banquet rooms offer 6,000 square feet of meeting space for up to 250 people. State-of-the-art audiovisual aids are available for speakers' presentations. A full-time message center keeps communication lines open and efficient for busy business guests.

To relax from business meetings, guests can take a dip in the hotel's 50-foot swimming pool or heated whirlpool spa or work out in a fitness facility with the most up-to-date exercise equipment. There is antique shopping in Lafayette and department store shopping in nearby Walnut Creek. San Francisco is just 25 miles away.

The hotel's restaurant, The Duck Club Restaurant, specializes in imaginative regional American cuisine. A wide-ranging dinner selection offers creative presentations of duck, veal, beef, chicken, fresh fish, and pasta. In addition, guests can usually find an array of game meats, fowl, and items reminiscent of the meals at the famous hunt clubs. Room service is available from 6 a.m. to 10 p.m.

Just off Highway 24 in Lafayette, the hotel is centrally located in the heart of Contra Costa County—two minutes from Walnut Creek and five minutes from Concord. Complimentary shuttle service takes guests to the business parks and commercial areas of the Highway 24-680 corridor and nearby Buchanan Field. Standard limousine service is available to the San Francisco, Oakland, and San Jose airports.

The Lafayette Park Hotel is owned and operated by the Western Lodging Group, a hotel management firm headquartered in

*The soundproof guest rooms feature king- or double-queen-size beds with carved cherrywood headboards and side tables, armoires that conceal color television sets, and comfortable sitting areas with large desks.*

Redwood City. The company also runs the Napa Valley Lodge, Bodega Bay Lodge, Half Moon Bay Lodge, and the Stanford Park Hotel in Menlo Park.

For those who want a luxurious taste of old-world elegance combined with a hearty serving of new-world convenience, the Lafayette Park Hotel may have just the menu.

# Concord Hilton

Foresight is an important quality in the hospitality industry—a hotel must be able to recognize the growth potential of a region and act decisively. In 1982 the owners of the Concord Hilton did just that, opening the full-service, business-oriented hotel just before the explosive growth of the Interstate 680 corridor in Contra Costa.

Over the past six years the Concord Hilton has catered to the needs of thousands of business travelers, hosting the conventions, conferences, and meetings of such major corporations as Dow Chemical, Chevron, and Bank of America. Numerous celebrities and their entourages have also stayed at the hotel, including Gerald Ford and Muhammed Ali, as well as many entertainers performing at the nearby Concord Pavilion—Liza Minelli, Bette Midler, and Eddie Money, to name only a few.

Today the Concord Hilton is still the leader in business travel and conferences in Contra Costa County, offering more meeting and banquet space than any other hotel in the Interstate 680 corridor. It has 14,000 square feet of professional meeting space for international business conferences and local group functions.

The main conference facility, the Golden Gate Ballroom, seats 1,100 theater-style or 850 for banquets and dinners. The three Park rooms can accommodate meetings, luncheons, or dinners for groups of 10 to 40—or the rooms can be combined to seat up to 120. The Executive Conference Center offers a luxurious environment for smaller seminars and functions.

The Hilton's five gracious hospitality suites are perfect for entertaining clients and hosting receptions. Regardless of the size or subject of the conference, state-of-the-art audiovisual technology is always available to enhance the quality of speakers' presentations.

For relaxation, the business traveler can take a dip in the pool or hop on a free shuttle to the Big C health club for a workout and sauna. Several professional-quality golf courses and tennis courts are also enticing options.

For evening entertainment, the Profiles cocktail lounge provides musical acts and a Casablanca ambience for renewing old acquaintances and getting to know new colleagues. The Plaza Court, overlooking the hotel's open-air courtyard, presents a casual afternoon piano bar and a complimentary continental breakfast for all business travelers.

The hotel's two restaurants, Pandanus and Poppy's Cafe, offer contrasting styles and menus, depending on the diner's needs and appetite. The Pandanus dinner menu features mesquite-grilled California cuisine in an elegant setting. Poppy's casual atmosphere and food selections make it ideal for breakfast or lunch.

During or after the conference, guests can see the sights of nearby San Francisco—only 45 minutes by car or BART—or the famed wine country of Napa Valley—only an hour away. The hotel is also a short drive from Silicon Valley and the state capital in Sacramento.

Hospitality is often forgotten in the hectic world of business travel, but not at the Concord Hilton. Since its opening in 1982 the facility has earned a solid reputation for efficient service and warm, friendly personnel. In an industry renowned for high employee turnover, one-third of the original staff is still with the hotel.

Despite its commercial success the Concord Hilton has never forgotten its community roots, donating to or making special arrangements for meeting space for many community, civic, and philanthropic organizations. The Concord Chamber of Commerce holds numerous functions at the hotel, including its Cinco de Mayo dance attended annu-

ally by 1,000 people. The Concord-Diablo Rotary Club meets weekly at the Hilton, and the Concord Rotary puts on its annual Big Board fund raiser there. As the host for the annual East Bay Food and Wine Experience, the hotel takes on the burden of a major fund-raising effort involving 1,500 guests.

For one day every year the Hilton hands over its kitchens and dining rooms to the students of the Diablo Valley College Hotel-Restaurant Management School, who prepare and serve their own annual awards dinner.

Last but certainly not least is the establishment's unique Adopt an Angel Christmas program, in which the staff distributes gifts, clothing, and food to 25 needy families in central Contra Costa.

The Concord Hilton, located at 1970 Diamond Boulevard, just off the Willow Pass Road exit of Interstate 680, offers free parking for more than 800 cars. The hotel's 11 floors house 330 spacious guest rooms, many with panoramic views of the surrounding Contra Costa hills. As for safety, the Hilton's modern fire-prevention system has long been recognized as one of the best in the Bay Area. Several local fire departments, in fact, use the structure as a model for training fire fighters on high-rise buildings.

The hotel is jointly owned by Campbell Estates of Honolulu, Hawaii, and Associated Inns & Restaurants Company of America (AIRCOA), headquartered in Englewood, Colorado. AIRCOA is the nation's largest privately held hotel management and development organization, operating more than 50 hotels, inns, resorts, condominium properties, and convention centers, including the Clarion and Wynfield chains, and many Hiltons and Sheratons nationwide. Employing 9,800 people and managing a total of 13,000 guest rooms, AIRCOA-owned and -operated facilities produced $300 million in revenues in 1987.

Expert and experienced management is the key to the success of any hotel, and the Concord Hilton is no exception. Its ability to anticipate the needs of the community and its guests will continue to be the hallmark of the hotel as it pioneers new ways to make business travel more productive and enjoyable.

*Over the past six years the Concord Hilton has catered to the needs of thousands of business travelers, hosting conventions, conferences, and meetings. Today the Concord Hilton is still the leader in business travel and conferences, offering more meeting and banquet space than any other hotel in the 680 corridor.*

These hikers enjoy an after-noon of climbing along the majestic slopes of Mount Diablo. Photo by Mark Gibson

# PATRONS

The following individuals, companies, and organizations have made a valuable commitment to the quality of this publication. Windsor Publications and the Concord Chamber of Commerce gratefully acknowledge their participation in *Contra Costa County: A Chronicle of Progress*.

Armstrong Lorenz Gilmour & Whalen*
Arthur Young & Company*
California and Hawaiian Sugar Company*
Central Bank*
Central Contra Costa Transit Authority*
Chevron Land and Development Company*
CONCO Cement Company*
Concord Hilton*
Concord TV Cable*
Contra Costa Community College District*
Contra Costa Council*
Contra Costa Water District*
Diablo Magazine*
Dow Chemical U.S.A.*
East Bay Municipal Utility District*
Jacuzzi Whirlpool Bath*
John F. Kennedy University*
KKIS AM/FM*
Lafayette Park Hotel*
Lesher Communications*
Longs Drugstores*
Los Medanos Community Hospital*
McCutchen, Doyle, Brown & Enersen*
Mason-McDuffie Insurance Service, Inc.*
Micropump Corporation*
Mt. Diablo Medical Center*
Pacific Gas & Electric*
Saint Mary's College*
Sun Valley Ford
Sunvalley Shopping Center*
Thiessen, Gagen & McCoy*
Trembath, McCabe, Schwartz, Evans & Levy*
Wentling Photography*

*Contra Costa's Enterprises in *Contra Costa County: A Chronicle of Progress*. The histories of these companies and organizations appear in Part Two, beginning on page 112

Alan, Maggie, and Nancy Nichols. "The Richest People of the East Bay." *Diablo: The Magazine of the East Bay.* Concord, 1987.

Andrews, Edna May. *History of Concord: Its Progress and Promise.* Concord Historical Society: Concord, 1986.

Association of Bay Area Governments' Perspectives 1987. Berkeley, 1987.

Bay Area Rapid Transit District 1987 Five Year Plan. Vol. 1. Oakland, 1987.

Contra Costa Community College District 1985 Report. Martinez, 1985.

*Contra Costa Times.* Issues of May 10, September 4, September 24, September 25, and December 15, 1987, and the Annual Report of January 1987. Walnut Creek, 1987.

*Focus on Housing: A Challenge of the '80s in Contra Costa County.* Contra Costa Council: San Ramon, 1986.

Growth Trends 1985. Contra Costa Community Development Department: Martinez, 1985.

Quarterly Report, Center for Real Estate and Urban Economics, University of California. Berkeley, 1987.

Saint Mary's College. A Viewbook of the College. Moraga, 1987.

Walnut Creek Area Chamber of Commerce. "Walnut Creek Business." Walnut Creek, December 1987.

# INDEX